OPAMS AND BUNDU BEETLES

Opams and Bundu Beetles

by

Blake Bromley

The Pentland Press Limited
Edinburgh · Cambridge · Durham · USA

© Blake Bromley 2000

First published in 2000 by
The Pentland Press Ltd.
1 Hutton Close
South Church
Bishop Auckland
Durham

All rights reserved.
Unauthorised duplication
contravenes existing laws.

British Library Cataloguing in Publication Data.
A catalogue record for this book is available
from the British Library.

ISBN 1 85821 740 7

Typeset by George Wishart & Associates, Whitley Bay.
Printed and bound by Bookcraft (Bath) Ltd.

To Beryl

who through brilliant research, found the lost generations of my mother's family. She read, corrected and made helpful suggestions throughout the gestation of this book.

My thanks to:

My mother-in-law, Mildred Whitehouse, at whose instigation I began to write this story.

My friends and family for their interest and encouragement throughout its writing.

My newly found third cousin, Anthony Armitage, for his generous gift of the photos of our shared two and three times great grandmothers.

Contents

Foreword xi

Introduction 1

England (1936)

1. Furlough 1

Part 1
A wartime Colonial Childhood

Malaya (1936-1942)

2. Alor Star 5
3. Mother's Family 9
4. Johore Bahru 16

India (1942-1945)

5. Refugees 29
6. Ootacamund 33
7. Mission Station 52
8. Coonoor 63
9. The End of the War 71
10. Deolali 76

Part 2
Post-war England through the eyes of a young boy

England (1946-1949)

11. Sailing Home 83
12. First Impressions 89

13. The Headmaster	97
14. The Norfolk Broads	106
15. Summer 1946	110
16. Christmas	121
17. The Terrible Winter of 1947	129
18. The Staff	133
19. Odds and Ends	137
20. Summer Holidays	150
21. Seasoned Schoolboy	161
22. Family Holiday	170
Postscript	179

List of Maps and Photographs

Map of Malaya	4
Julie Marie Jumeaux (née Migot-de-la-Combe)	10
Susan Jumeaux (née Armitage) and some of her children	11
Allan Jumeaux with his second wife and extended family	14
Harvey in Chinese outfit and Blake in fez and sarong	23
Map of India	28
Schoolboys in India, 1942, just before their sixth and seventh birthdays	36
Mission Station, Koyallagudem	58
Eustace Blake Bromley and Anna Elizabeth	60
The re-united family one year after the end of the war	119
Schoolfriends at Eversfield	145
Blake, Harvey, Else and the horse	175

Foreword
by Pamela Kay

As we prepared to leave Calcutta, a violent thunderstorm of monsoon ferocity broke over the *Minerva*. Dramatic lightning and sheeting rain accompanied our cruise ship as she sailed down the Hooghly. The rain lifted and very gradually the sun began to disperse the sodden clouds. We made our way to the sun-loungers on deck and Blake Bromley, who by chance was sitting next to me, said that he was delighted to be here again after fifty-two years.

'I have not been back since I was a schoolboy. When I broke my leg a few months ago and had nothing else to do, I started to write a book about my childhood,' he said, his smiling face revealing all. Clearly there was much more to come. 'Wonderful,' I remember saying (and thinking, I do hope he will finish it). 'I would love to read it. *Please do get on with it,*' I told him, fairly sternly.

My husband had been in the Indian Army and had spent a great deal of time in the Far East. There were many on board who, like us, were making a nostalgic journey (in greater comfort) re-visiting the places of their past. I had never been to India before, but had experienced it second-hand through my husband, who gave me Hindi lessons over breakfast on board.

I had become more and more immersed in, and fascinated by, the lives and stories of people who had lived there. Blake's total recall of his early life in India describes with almost surreal clarity the colour, atmosphere and light of the India that I was to glimpse on that memorable voyage down the east coast to Orrissa and Madras.

Although his experience was of an earlier time, India moves slowly. With the insidious growth of satellite TV, India is changing. It is vital that personal experiences, memories and family history are preserved – life as it really was – although rarely described as evocatively as this.

It is not often that a brief conversation with a man who was then a perfect stranger, should result in such riches.

Pamela Kay ARCA RWS RBA NEAC

Pamela Kay is one of Britain's most popular working artists with a hugely successful sequence of one-woman exhibitions throughout the past two decades.

Introduction

ENGLAND
(1936)

1. Furlough

It must have been one of those ironies of life that I was born at the height of a snow storm on 17 January 1936 at 61 Weldon Crescent, a small nursing home in Harrow, a suburb of London. My mother had never seen snow, had never lived anywhere but in tropical Malaya and, shortly thereafter, we would live for the next ten years of my life in the heat of the Far East. I had been born in the last three days of King George V's reign and had just qualified as a Georgian.

My father was a young English Colonial Civil Servant schoolmaster who had gone out to Malaya in 1931 and it was there that he met and subsequently married my mother. My expected arrival was due during one of my father's six month periods of furlough which came round initially after four years' service and thereafter every three years or so; with no appreciation of the upheaval, both physical and emotional, which the birth of a baby would cause, he decided to take my pregnant mother to visit Britain and Europe. Shortly after my birth, they embarked on the long train journey to visit his many German relatives from his mother's side and then, travelling by way of Switzerland, they visited friends in the south of France whom Father had known during his student days. There were no clothes washing facilities on the trains and Mother ran out of nappies for me and had to resort to Father's handkerchiefs, presumably padded with cotton wool. There were no tissues or disposable nappies in those days.

My brother Harvey was born in Kuala Lumpur a year and a fortnight after me and my sister Else was a post-war afterthought, twelve years younger than me, also born in Malaya. Harvey and I would share our experiences until I left school at the age of eighteen.

Part 1

**A WARTIME
COLONIAL CHILDHOOD**

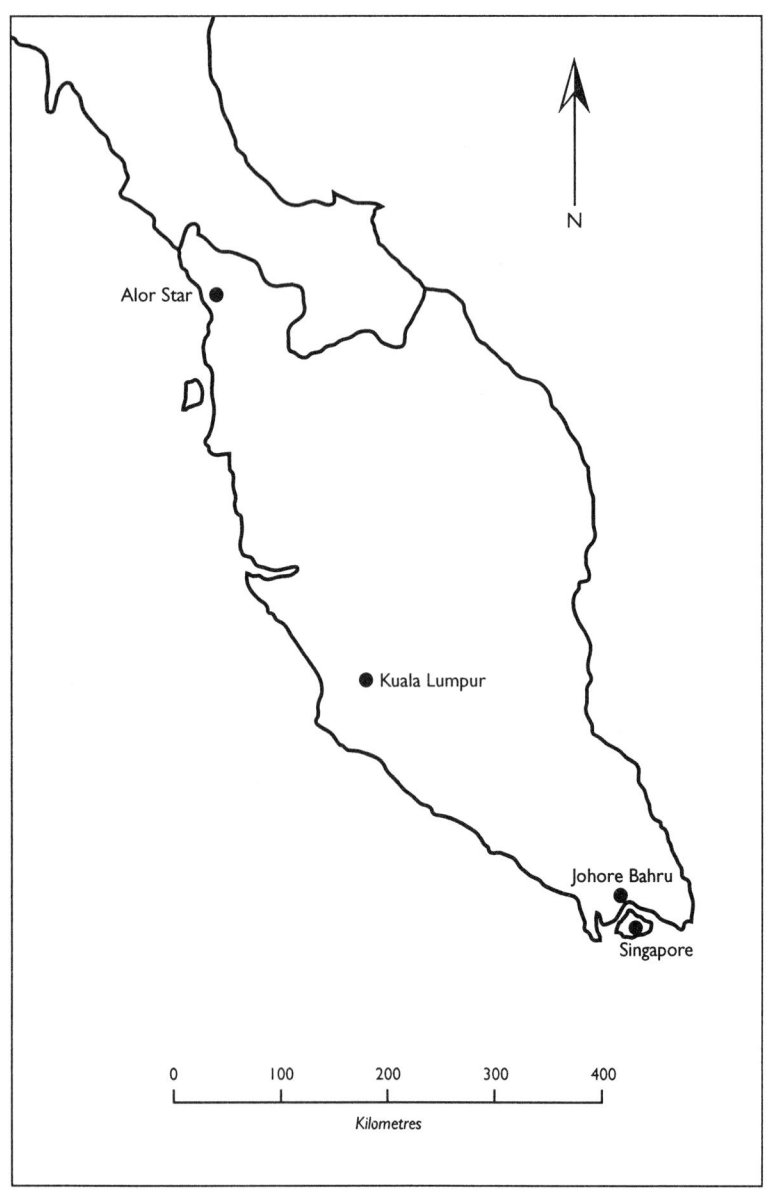

Map of Malaya.

MALAYA
(1936-1942)

2. Alor Star

My earliest recollections are of being taken for walks to the local golf course by Amah, our Chinese nurse. My brother Harvey would have been about eighteen months old and he would sit in state in the pram while I had to walk. I felt a keen sense of resentment at this unfair treatment of a two and a half year old. The first car that registered in my memory was a pre-war Ford V8 that was parked along the route of one of these walks. I can still see it vividly in my mind after almost sixty years.

For those first three years, we lived in Alor Star and memories are few. I have a selective memory of parts of the house with a covered walkway to the detached kitchen and servants' quarters at the back: meals had to be carried from there into the house. We had a cook and gardener, as well as Amah, and a house-servant, who served at mealtimes and kept our home clean. We also had a dog called 'Wheskit', a small to medium size mongrel bitch with a black and white waistcoat marking. I was told that when I was three years old and she had just had puppies, I collected them in the basket of my tricycle and rode around the house posting them in each of the rooms in simulation of the local newspaper boy on his delivery round. Their distressed squeals and the frantic barks of their mother brought my mother rushing to the rescue.

Perhaps the most vivid memory of that time was of the stupendous monsoon rains with their unbroken streams – as though someone was pouring water from a cosmic sized watering can – the evocative smells of newly wet earth and the scorched smell of electric discharges after the lightning strikes; the sounds of thunderclaps; the continuous drumming on the roof and the churned water surfaces with their high rebound. We would sail our paper boats down the rapids of the overflowing gutters, watching them ducking and bobbing as they swirled away.

I also remember going on holiday to Kedah Peak, the local hill station at an altitude of 3,000 feet, and of being carried up, by native coolies, to the government Rest House in open wickerwork cane chairs slung on poles. The Rest House was of wooden construction with typical government issue furniture of cane and rattan chairs and tables and, on one of these tables, Dad had set out his work which included a set of drawing instruments, of which I particularly remember the set squares and ruler he used. It was there that I saw a centipede six inches long, flaming orange-red and translucent, weaving sinuously and swiftly along the jungle floor. Mother had told us that she had been in agony for days when a similar centipede, with poisonous feet, had crawled across her while she was asleep as a child. We often saw dark-brown or black millipedes this length and fatter than a man's thumb but they were slow and harmless.

On another occasion when we were back in Alor Star, a travelling Tamil magician put on a show on the front veranda and miraculously produced delicious savoury balls, the size of peas, from under cups in a variation of the three card trick. My mother must have been horrified to see us eat them in such unhygienic circumstances.

The dangers of wartime submarine attacks meant that in 1940 my father could not take his six months' leave in England and the family went first to India, to visit my missionary grandparents, and then to Australia and New Zealand via Ceylon. On the voyage to India, one bedtime I sat up suddenly

Alor Star

from my bunk and gashed my eyebrow on the pointed base of the bulkhead light and had to have two stitches inserted by the ship's doctor: the first of many thereafter. Even though I was so young at the time, the details remain with me, including the blue night-light bulb which illuminated the cabin throughout the hours of darkness. As a boy just after the war, I was told the names of the ships on which we travelled: the *Rawalpindi* on the way to India and torpedoed shortly after, and the *Strathaird* going from India to Australia. According to my grandfather's diaries, it was between 31 March and 17 April 1940 that we visited him and my grandmother at their mission station in Koyyalagudem in the Godavari district of India. It was in the compound of this mission station, to the terror of my parents, that I was reputed to have laid into a water buffalo from the milking herd with a ping-pong bat. The buffalo remained completely passive throughout and the effect of the blows was probably much less impressive than the noise of the bat. These buffaloes were far more tolerant of very young children, who were often put in charge of them, than they were of adults.

Likewise, only a few memories of Australia and New Zealand remain. There was the snowball Dad brought back in a thermos flask from Mount Wellington in Tasmania. The incident of my splitting my head by falling over the parapet of an empty fountain while walking backwards watching an aeroplane – this required six stitches. The most impressive spectacle of seeing the greater part of Britain's ocean liners, including *Queen Mary* and *Queen Elizabeth*, in wartime grey anchored off the Western Australian coast near Perth and filling the whole horizon. *Queen Elizabeth* had not yet seen passenger service at the time. The long journey when we travelled in a red coloured train in a sleeping compartment across the miles of Australia's red desert. There were two further incidents: one of me disgracing myself in the Sunday Morning Meeting by messing my trousers and Dad eventually determining the source of the smell and hauling me out not too gently; and the other, that of the sightseeing tour on the Sidney harbour ferry when over the public address system, in the startling tones of my own voice, came the words 'Hello Mummy!' I was the small boy who had seized his opportunity when the tour guide had gone to lunch and had left the microphone unattended. My final memory was of being phoned by Mum and Dad when they had gone to the mountains and we had been left at the guest-house; and of my then creeping down in the dark to try to ring them back from the hall phone and the resultant anger of the owner when he caught me talking to the operator on the town exchange. The lady operator must have realised that she was talking to a small child but the owner of the guest-house could only have been wondering what long distance phone bills I had run up on his behalf.

3. Mother's Family

Johore Bahru was our next home on our return to Malaya. Whereas Alor Star was at the extreme north of the country, Johore was as far south as you could go and was about 450 miles from Alor Star. My mother's parents lived in Kuala Lumpur which was about halfway up the country, equidistant between Alor Star and Johore, and we visited them regularly.

Mother's family was a large one headed by my grandfather, blind in his old age, and bearing the strange name of Jumeaux. His pedigree on his father's side went back to France at the time of the French revolution, where the family account states that his great great grandfather, Antoine Louis Migot-de-la-Combe, was a Lieutenant in the 'Garde de Luxembourg', which formed the bodyguard of King Louis and Queen Marie Antoinette. When the King and Queen were arrested after their attempted flight out of the country, Antoine fled with his wife to Holland. He may have remained there until after the period of the Terror but they eventually made their way south via Switzerland and boarded a ship at Marseille for India and a new life.

Antoine's daughter, my three times great grandmother, was born in 1799 and had the wonderful name of Julie Marie Josephine Eléanor Migot-de-la-Combe. She married John Pierre Jumeaux, also the son of French refugees. In 1817, a year or so after their marriage, they moved to live in Ceylon and John was subsequently appointed Fiscal of the Western Province in 1839. Their son Louis followed him in becoming a district judge and

Julie Marie Josephine Eléanor Jumeaux (née Migot-de-la-Combe) born 1799, my three times great grandmother, and the daughter of the Lieutenant who fled the French Revolution. He was in King Louis XVI's palace guard.

married Susan Armitage, daughter of a Lancashire cotton-mill owner. She had gone out to Ceylon to join her merchant venturer brothers. John, the eldest of them, had already married Louis' sister Fanny Henriette. Both couples had large families, but tragically both Susan and Louis died of malaria within eighteen months of each other.

The old lady, their grandmother Julie Marie, who had been living with the family in Ceylon, had to assume charge of the orphaned youngsters and, in the last months of 1862, aged sixty

Mother's Family

My two times great grandmother, Susan (née Armitage), wife of Louis Jumeaux and some of her children. Taken in Ceylon c.1858. My great grandfather Arthur is seated.

three, take them all with the exception my great grandfather Arthur, on the long voyage to England aboard a windjammer, making an overland crossing from Port Suez to Port Said on the Mediterranean. The Suez canal had not yet been built at that time. Arthur was about fifteen and had not joined them because he was already destined for the Ceylon Civil Service, which he entered as a Magistrate at the age of eighteen. On disembarking, the family spent their first night in a London hotel before continuing with their journey to relatives in Manchester. When the children came down to their breakfast that morning, much to the astonishment of the other hotel guests, they turned around on the landing at the head of the staircase and came down backwards, holding on to the banisters. They had been at sea for so long that they had been indoctrinated in the technique as a safe means of descending the near vertical companionways between the decks and had not yet thrown off the habit.

Arthur, my great grandfather, died in his late twenties leaving a widow and six children. Arthur had married Harriet Lydia Thomasz, the daughter of a Burgher family of mixed race descent from Ceylon. The surname Thomasz, in itself, suggests a Portuguese origin. He would have broken all the conventions of Victorian society in marrying this Eurasian girl. Burgher families were formed from marriages between a European colonial and an Asian; they were ostracised by both communities and would then generally only be able to marry amongst themselves. The scandal probably led to his being cut off by the rest of his family, who were now in England, and this would have been further compounded by his very early death. Present generations of the English branch of the family talked for years of a 'Lost Uncle', and contact between the separate strands of the family has only recently been re-established.

My grandfather had lived with his mother and sisters but, because of the need to support them, he left Ceylon, while still a young man, to take up the opportunities that arose from the opening up of Malaya. He was a retired Civil Engineer who had gained his qualifications through City and Guilds College, London, and he had been very much involved in the early development of the infrastructure of the Malayan Peninsula. His blindness occurred very late in his life and was unusual in that he had asked for his eyes to be removed surgically. They were giving him very intense pain and, because the Malayan doctors of that time were unable to treat his condition, this solution remained the only one left to him. He had been given glass eyes with which he would occasionally frighten us by removing one and leaving it on a prominent ledge, where it would look out on our activities making sure that we were behaving ourselves. At least that is what he said it was doing: I am not sure that we believed him! He would sit us boys on his knees and would keep us enthralled with his many tales of encounters with wild animals in the jungle and stories of natives running amok when he was building roads through the then virgin rainforest. These stories would be accompanied by the appropriate roars or other jungle noises which would send us running out of the room in fear, only to then creep slowly back for more.

Besides my grandparents, the family consisted of four boys and four girls of which Mother and two boys were from grandfather's first wife and the others were half brothers and sisters. They were all very close knit, and none lived far away, providing Harvey and me with lots of uncles and aunts. Mother had a stepmother, known as Granny to us who, most unusually, was the niece of Mother's real mother, who had died exactly a year after Mum was born in 1906.

Our visits to Kuala Lumpur conjure up memories of Uncle Claude's brand new MG sports car; of my mother's three very pretty young sisters with their distinctly French looks and French names, Ouida, Sybil and Elise – Elise was still a teenager; of walks to the flat paddy fields interspersed with gigantic floating bucket dredgers excavating tin ore from vast lakes that they themselves had created.

The younger half of Mother's family, the half sisters who were as yet unmarried, lived with my grandparents; and their home, a large colonial bungalow, was forever being visited by the older married brothers and their families. Grandpa would have been in his late sixties then and seemed, despite his blindness, to thrive on the constant bustle. Badminton was a favourite activity played on the lawn and it was from this lawn that my stepgranny, relaxing in a deck chair in the shade, sent me indoors to find out the time. I, at four, was very proud of my newly acquired ability to read the time but, on this occasion, I came back very crestfallen to say to Granny that I could not tell her the time, because the clock was a Roman Catholic clock! I had not yet learnt my Roman numerals.

My grandfather Allan Jumeaux with his second wife and extended family. Photo taken in 1920, with my mother at 16 standing centre back row.

There was another granny here whom we called Granny Leach, who was my mother's step grandmother: really grandmother to mother's half sisters but because of the relationship of grandfather's first and second wives, she was also my mother's aunt. She seemed incredibly old and wizened and the fascination for us was the huge, very dark mole, with whiskers emanating from it, which grew on the side of her cheek and also the clothes she wore which were a relic from the previous generation and were invariably black or very dark brown.

One of the highlights of Kuala Lumpur was the breakfasts which often consisted of the whole family going out to the local street vendors to eat 'Opams' straight from the searing hot griddle on which the batter had been dropped. They were a sort of aerated crêpe made from rice flour with the yoke of an egg placed in its centre like a yellow eye.

It was here that I first came across *lalang*, the lethal grass which grew in profusion in the wild, provided there was open space, and it could grow very tall. I grabbed a handful to pull out for some reason and the next thing I knew, I had cut my hand very deeply and was bleeding all over my clothes. The edges of each grass blade were covered in microscopic barbs which acted as a very fine saw and these cut you as easily as a razor, leaving you unaware of what had happened. It was only afterwards, when you moved your fingers and this action opened up the cut, that it became quite painful. If it had been any deeper I would have required stitches.

Many were the expeditions from Kuala Lumpur. Sometimes these were to Batu Caves, huge underground limestone caverns with a river running through; sometimes to the Cameron Highlands, the local hill station 5,000 feet up, where it was cool enough for nature to be manipulated to resemble a microcosm of England with dairy cattle and strawberries, though if you went a few yards beyond man's interference, you were back in dense tropical jungle. At that period, the war had not impacted on Malaya and people carried on as they had in peacetime as though there was no shortage of petrol.

4. Johore Bahru

Johore Bahru was a small town on the extreme tip of the Malayan mainland from which ran the causeway which connected with the island of Singapore across the narrow Straits-of-Johore. Johore was one of the states of Malaya and our favourite walk from this new home was to the palace gardens of the Sultan of Johore, the ruler of the state, where he kept a small zoo. The road to the zoo had just been resurfaced and I enjoyed stooping down and popping the bubbles of soft tar with my forefinger, much to the concern of Amah, who afterwards had the unenviable task of cleaning our hands and anything else that we had touched with them. Another of our favourite haunts was the sandy beach on the strait, where the tide ran fast between the island and the mainland. A group of us European children would regularly go there with our Amahs and on one occasion, when all the Amahs were engrossed in conversation amongst themselves, we managed to board a tethered sampan, floating about knee deep, and cast off without their noticing. As we drifted out we eventually realised that we were being caught by the current and I, as the oldest of the group and the ringleader, shouted 'Jump!' and we all jumped out. The younger children were up to their necks and the Amahs, who by now had heard the screams of alarm, had to rush into the water to rescue the little ones and to swim out to the boat to recover it. I think it was on this occasion, when waiting for retribution from my father that, on hearing his car arrive, I ran into the darkness of

Johore Bahru

the bedroom and hid under the bed, not knowing that my feet were sticking out. It did not take Dad very long to find me and haul me out. The ensuing spanking was well justified.

Harvey and I, as sons of an English Colonial official, had the natural forwardness of youngsters born to the authority that came with Empire and we got away with murder with our long-suffering Amah. There seemed to be few of the curbs that we would have experienced in England. We could be wild and, later in India, we could wander wherever we liked unsupervised.

There was the occasion when we tied a washing line across the room securely anchored at one end to a full height solid teak cloaks cupboard and at the other to the window frame. After climbing onto the table we swung out hand over hand in the manner of Tarzan crossing a ravine, much to the amusement of Amah, who was squatting in the Chinese fashion indulgently watching the eccentric antics of her charges. Suddenly, it must have been the addition of the weight of the second one of us, the cloaks cupboard fell with a huge crash across Amah's thigh. Amazingly her leg was not broken but she was very badly bruised and in severe pain. Such was her loyalty to us that she would not let on to Mum, who only discovered her injuries later when she saw her flinching. There was the time when we improvised a roundabout by tying a washing line to the huge ceiling fans that colonial houses had and then, with Harvey hanging on, I flicked the switch. I do not recall what happened but probably we ruined the mechanism of the fan. Amah was fully aware of what we were doing but never thought to stop us. She was so compliant that we persuaded her to enter a large camphorwood linen chest as part of one of our imaginary games. Mum came rushing out to her screams to find us poking her with a walking stick through the remaining unclosed gap between the box and the lid. We were imitating the sword trick that we had recently seen carried out by a local itinerant magician. In it a young girl was put in a wicker basket and after closing the lid the magician then proceeded to poke swords through the basket. Needless to say, in the real trick, no harm came to the young girl. Fortunately all these escapades occurred when Dad was at work and I don't think Mum told him unless the damage was too serious to be hidden.

I was told some years later that as youngsters we had picked up both Malay and Chinese from the servants and that Amah thought of us as her surrogate children. No wonder she did not report us. Though I have pretty well forgotten most of it, and certainly all my Chinese, my wife is amazed at the number of Malay and Indian words that I still come out with nowadays, though I am usually unaware that I have said them.

Our home was a happy one. We did not see a lot of Dad except in the holidays. He was the son of missionaries in India and had been brought up at boarding school, first in India and then in England and, following a very good mathematics degree at Bristol University and teacher training in London, he went out as a teacher to Malaya. His christian names were Eustace Hans: one English and one German, in recognition of his mixed English and German parentage; but his German name Hans was the one by which he was known. All his five brothers and sisters were similarly given a name from each nationality. His non-conformist parents brought him up in the Plymouth Brethren tradition and he was a practising Christian. With this background, it was not surprising that he was fairly adventurous and we as a family travelled on every possible occasion. He was also a keen ornithologist and was always going off with likeminded friends to jungle camps to birdwatch. He was the proud possessor of a pre-war Austin 12, the family car used on our travels, and his other treasured possession was his 'His Master's Voice' gramophone, with its enormous horn and its mahogany cabinet. Accompanying this he had a large collection of classical 78 r.p.m. records and he and Mother would spend many an evening listening to concertos and symphonies, interrupted by the frequent need to change the records or replace the needle.

Iris, my mother's name, was intended as French but everyone pronounced it the English way. She had an indomitable spirit of which she was going to have great need in the years to come. She was tiny, just four foot ten and dainty; but she had a wiry stamina that belied her small stature and, like her sisters, she had those distinctly French looks which centred round her dark brown eyes. She was a very sweet-natured and happy person who always put others first and she had a very deep Christian faith which she practised in everything she did, though never imposing her beliefs on others. She had also been brought up in the Plymouth Brethren tradition and it was at meetings in their Assembly Hall at Kuala Lumpur that she first met my father. The Plymouth Brethren were a group of Christians who believed that they should attempt to follow the practices of the early church, with no formal ecclesiastical organisation, in a simple faith sharing with one another as equals, much as the Quakers do now. Their services were unstructured with long silences interspersed with individuals saying a prayer, or announcing a hymn, or reading from God's word, or developing a thought from the bible reading, each as they felt moved to express their feelings. The singing was unaccompanied and relied on the services of a brother to pitch the tune with sometimes questionable success. Only the men could take an active part in these services and one of their peculiarities was that the women had to wear hats in the meetings, in strict adherence to St Paul's admonition that women should have their heads covered.

Mother trained and worked as a secretary but gave it up on marriage and she was also a very accomplished needlewoman and knitter. She made most of her own dresses which never looked homemade. She had a quiet influence on us boys and we owe a great deal to her. One quirk she had was to make us stand on tiptoe fifty times a day to develop our arches so that we would not get flat feet. She had no end of small knick-knacks that fascinated us including an egg turned from yellow boxwood, the two halves fitting tightly together like those in Russian doll sets, in which she kept her sewing needles. But by far the most interesting of her treasures was a camphorwood promise box, about the size of a small cigar box, filled with tightly rolled cylinders of paper about an inch wide, each of which when unrolled had a text or promise from the Bible. The effect of looking down on the box was that of an end-on view of a tin of cigarettes where all the tobacco was missing. The idea of the box was that you picked one out, a sort of lucky dip, and saw what God's promise was for you that day. We boys were not satisfied with one promise for the day, we liked lots, and the real fun was rolling them all up again and putting them back in the box. Mother's sewing table with all its drawers and compartments full of multicoloured cotton reels, thimbles, a conch shell for darning socks, scissors, binding tape etc., was another source of entertainment; though how she found anything again after we had been at it remains a mystery. She was also very adept at origami and taught us how to make a variety of paper models of which the sailing and double hulled boats were our favourites.

My parents entertained a fair bit without going to excess. They often had parties for servicemen and women who had come to their local and very lively church and I remember the frustration of being put to bed just when things were getting into full swing. They also had the Brethren practice of inviting people to lunch who had nowhere else to go after the Sunday morning service.

Our beds gave us an enormous sense of security as we lay surrounded by an all enveloping mosquito net. The world was shut out and nothing could possibly harm us. I did have one recurring dream from which I always woke up in a pouring sweat, only to find instant relief on seeing my mosquito net

Johore Bahru

intact. I would dream that I was desperately swimming to shore in a slowly moving river and never getting anywhere and that a bloated carcass of a dog was drifting down onto me. I would always wake up just before it touched me. The origin of this dream must have been from seeing an actual carcass in the river on one of our daily walks.

From our beds we could watch the geckos running up the walls and across the ceiling, clinging on upside down with specially adapted feet to enable them to achieve this apparently impossible task. These were small brown-green lizards about six inches long which, if you attempted to catch them by the tail, left it wriggling in your hand while they ran off to grow another tail in about six weeks or so. Strangely enough the new tail grew alongside the stump of the original and gave them a lopsided look that told you that this one had been caught before.

Car journeys, when we went on holiday, were initially of great interest as we passed through a succession of paddy fields, rubber plantations, jungle and villages. We would see the patient Chinese women progressing slowly across the field planting out the rice, for invariably it would be the Chinese who worked in the paddy fields, stooped double, as they stood in echelon in six inches of water so as to give themselves more working space between each other; with their conical raffia sun hats gently bobbing to the rhythm. We also saw the rubber tappers, generally Tamils, with their parangs, cutting chevron grooves and a central collecting channel into the bark of the trees and placing a cup at the base to collect the latex as it oozed downwards. Then there would be several crossings on pontoon ferries across wide rivers, always near the mouth of the river where it discharged into the sea. This was because the main arterial roads up and down the length of Malaya ran close to the sea on the coastal plain to avoid the spine of mountains inland. The cars would have to be driven up ramps onto the ferries, which would require some skill by the driver. For us children the distances travelled on these journeys would seem so great that eventually we could not take any more excitement and we would get bored and eventually fall asleep.

There were four distinct nationalities with whom we came into contact. Making the usual broad generalisations, these were: Europeans, always in positions of relative authority; Chinese, like Amah, who were very industrious and adaptable and took on all sorts of roles as domestic servants, or as coolies or as peasants who often worked in the paddy fields and who were great vegetable gardeners when working in their own plots or in the case of the better educated ones, working in commerce or in the professions; Indians, mainly Tamils, working as shopkeepers and clerks and who provided the bulk of the labour force for the rubber plantations; and Malays who tended to live in the rural villages called kampongs, where they were more or less self sufficient. Malays also provided the backbone of the police force where they were very disciplined and liked to wear their smart service uniform, which may have been an overspill from the neat sarong and fez clothing they wore in the kampongs. This contrasted with their otherwise happy-go-lucky nature, which made them disinclined to do any more work than was absolutely necessary. The Malays would occasionally become moody and were known to run amok, and when this happened, they could knife people for imagined slights: but generally they were very cheerful. I had a Malay sarong and fez and Harvey had a Chinese outfit in which we attended children's parties and we both have formal photographs of these costumes taken at that time. In the main, the Malays were Muslim; the Chinese were ancestor worshippers, though many had been converted to Christianity; the Tamils were Hindus and the Europeans were at least nominally Christian. The whole melting pot seemed to work well, at least in pre-war days.

Construction activities always interested us; probably to the annoyance of the workmen who would be asked innumerable

Johore Bahru

*Harvey (left) dressed in a Chinese outfit and
Blake as a Malay, dressed in fez and sarong.*

questions about what they were doing. One such project was the swing Dad ordered for us, which was the old fashioned type: not a sensible 'A' frame as now, but one with two vertical poles and a crossbar from which the ropes and seat hung. Dad insisted that we waited three days for the ground to consolidate before we used it. Even so it soon began to rock in its foundations with a repetitive thump. As the war drew closer to Malaya it became essential to construct an Anderson shelter at the bottom of the garden and this was another project which was a source of great attraction to us boys as we watched its progress.

I was due to start school and I had just learnt to ride a bike, pushed by one of the servants round the garden, when war postponed one and curtailed the other. I had even been to the school and seen my place setting in the dining hall with the serviette ring that I was to use. It was in the shape of a jade green duck with a black eye. Well before this, however, Mother had bought a blackboard and chalks and some primers and I had learnt to read; which proved to be very farsighted, as it would be a long time before I received a formal education.

It was about this time that I discovered Dad's camera, a Reflex Korelli taking a full $2^1/4$" square roll film. It was a single lens reflex which, before the war, was pretty rare and it had a ground glass viewing screen: no pentaprism in those days. The image passed through the lens and reflected off a 45° mirror onto the screen. The arrangement was much like a modern Hasselblad camera, with fold down shutters that sprang up on the four sides of the screen to protect it from unwanted light, which was further excluded from above by one's face peering down into it. When the shutter release was pressed, there was a pleasing thump as the mirror was raised before the shutter clicked. Long exposure settings of one second made a nice buzz and the remote shutter release gave an even longer buzz. Closing the four viewfinder shutters in sequence with a final click was very satisfying. It was also of great interest to turn the focusing ring and watch the image move in and out of focus. On the other hand the diaphragm stops did not seem to do much except to darken the image. It was a tribute to Dad that he did not go mad when he saw me playing with it and in all probability there was no film in it at the time.

I first learned of the start of the war because of the nervous chatter and stir of apprehension amongst the adult members of my mother's extended family on the very day we went to Batu Caves. We were at Kuala Lumpur on holiday and I could have been only three at the time, so that none of this meant very much to me. The day the Japanese invaded Malaya was a different matter. I was five and I clearly remember Father coming home and discussing it with my married uncles and aunts who were staying with us at the time, and the concern and worry on their faces. Soon afterwards, Father joined up with the Johore

Johore Bahru

Volunteers as a sapper and asked to be put in a non-combatant role, which resulted in him being placed in the cookhouse. We only saw him occasionally at weekends after that. I think it was on this same day of invasion that the last big motor race in Malaya was taking place in the pouring rain and the adults were listening to the radio commentary. I remember their discussing the madness of racing under these conditions and their horror as the commentator, with mounting excitement, began to report a serious accident in which two cars had gone off the road at great speed and one of the drivers had been killed.

Christmas 1941 was a very subdued affair. The Japanese had started to bomb Singapore and, with our house on a hill, we could look across to the island. One night, we watched as huge fires of dense black smoke and orange flames engulfed the oil storage tanks which had been hit; and these continued to burn for days. We could hear the crump of the bombs on the city even at that range. Dad was allowed home on Christmas Eve and for Christmas Day and he brought us the most wonderful present: a Hornby 'O'-gauge clockwork train set with a small tank engine and two trucks running on a circular track. We played with it almost continuously: little did we know that in six weeks' time we would have lost everything.

Another night, when the air raid sirens sounded, I was in the bath and Mum told us all to hurry down to the shelter. The bathroom had a small wooden duckboard to step onto and, what with being soapy, I slipped as I climbed out and I caught the edge of the duckboard with my foot. This made it spin up and, as I fell, the sharp corner of the board slit a one inch gash in my ear. I was rushed to hospital and had four stitches. I had now had fourteen stitches before the age of six. One benefit of this fall was that one of my aunts gave me a *Tiny Tim* comic annual to read in hospital where I was kept overnight.

Towards the end of January, some of my mother's family had fled from the advancing Japanese as they moved south and were staying with us. I remember them discussing the possibility of getting a ship to flee the country. Unfortunately for them, because they were not British passport holders, they were unable to do so but, because Dad was English, Mum, Harvey and I were eventually given passage on one of the last ships to leave Singapore in the first week of February 1942. The ship was the *Felix Rousell*, a French ship constructed in haste as a wartime utility ship, presumably before France fell, and it had the unlikely feature of square funnels as a consequence. She was painted in wartime grey.

It was a sad farewell. Uncle Claude drove us to the docks and Dad was allowed just enough time away from his unit to join us for one or two hours before we left. It was the last we saw of him for more than three and a half years. We had to leave everything behind and Mum had the equivalent of threepence in her purse with which to face the journey and a new country.

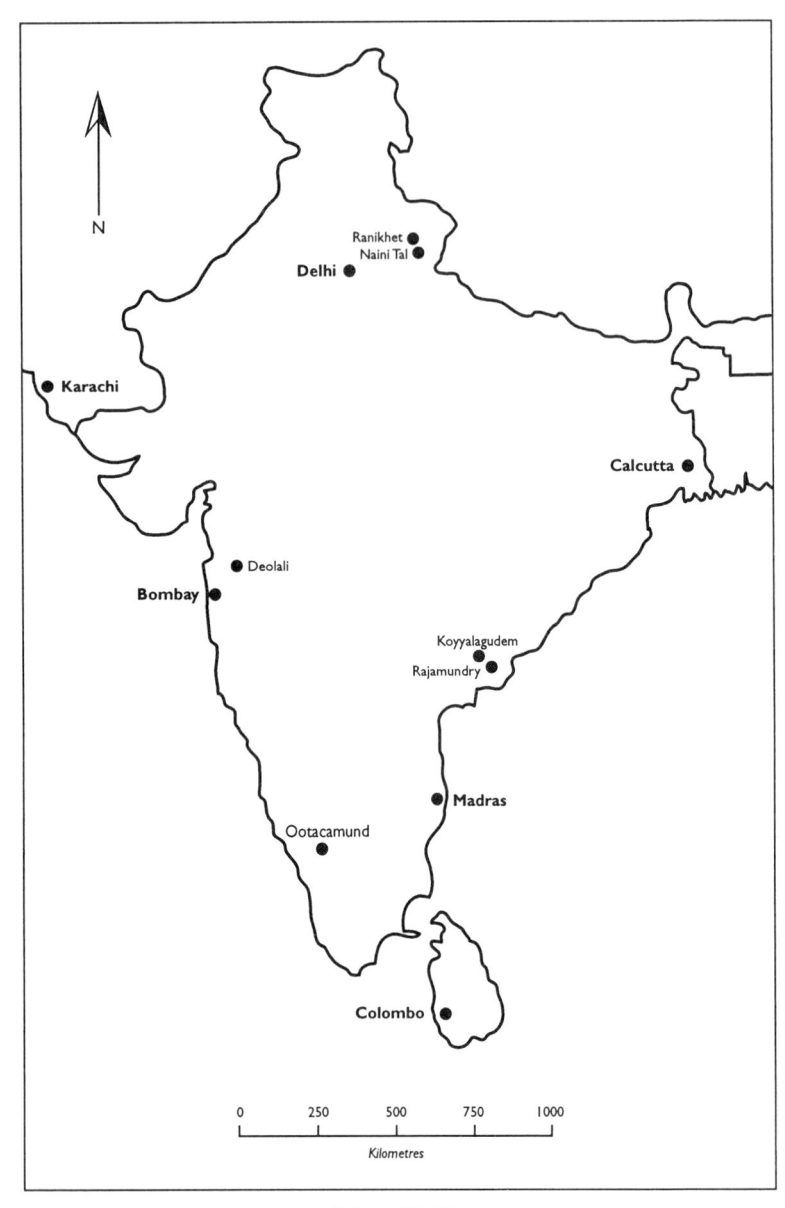

Map of India.

INDIA
(1942–1945)

5. Refugees

The *Felix Rousell* was bound for India, as no ships were then being allowed to go back to England because of the very real danger of being torpedoed. The ship was jam packed with refugees sleeping wherever they could find a space below decks. Food was brought in a galvanised iron bathtub to collection points in the sleeping areas and then it was a free-for-all. Mother would collect enough for the two of us in the one bowl she was issued with but by the time she went back for her own share there would be nothing left. She became so underfed, as she ate virtually nothing for the whole voyage, that one day she fainted and when she came round, she found Harvey and me crying over her because we thought she was dead.

The ship was attacked several times by Japanese aircraft and at the first hint of an attack, everyone who was not ship's crew was sent down into the bowels of the ship below the waterline, where it was hoped that bombs would not penetrate. In fact this would have been a death trap if a submarine had been in the vicinity and launched a torpedo. After the all-clear, the youngsters on the ship would rush up on deck and collect all the empty brass casings from the anti-aircraft machine guns, from the scuppers, or from where they had ended up as they rolled about on deck. These were the only toys we had and it was amazing what our fertile imaginations could make them become. Despite all the attacks, we eventually made it to Bombay on the west coast of India where it was much safer from

Japanese submarines than it would have been if we had gone to a port in the Bay of Bengal.

All the refugees from the ship were immediately put onto trains and sent on the long journey to the north-east of the country into the foothills of the Himalayas, a distance of about a thousand miles. The last part of the journey was completed by bus and the views as we got closer and closer to the distant snowclad mountains became increasingly spectacular until finally we were in amongst them at a tiny hamlet called Ranikhet. This consisted of not much more than the native village and a few stone huts used by the army. We were in the army huts, with no heating and very little bedding, and it was so cold that Mum developed frostbite which required treatment for a considerable time afterwards. She had, in her usual selflessness, given us most of her blankets. I think we were at an altitude of at least five to six thousand feet in conifer and mixed deciduous forest, a haven for wild animals. It was known that there was a panther in the neighbourhood and the jungle noises at night were alarming. One night we awoke to hear a big cat prowling around the huts and making a deep-throated growling noise and we two boys were terrified that it would break in through the wooden door. Mother quickly moved us into the same bunk and then lay on top of us, I suspect to calm us rather than to provide any material protection. Nevertheless it was an incredibly brave action and next morning the pug marks of a small leopard or panther were visible in the muddy surroundings. It is doubtful that these animals would take anyone from inside a hut but that made it no less an ordeal for us.

We were soon moved to the neighbouring hill station of Naini Tal, a popular place for Europeans to escape the heat of the plains during the hot season and it was famous for its vast lake nestling in a bowl of the mountains. It was here, while we were watching the kites circling round the sky and I was on a balcony of the house eating Ryvita with Marmite, that suddenly there was a whooshing noise and I experienced a sharp pain in my finger, which began to bleed steadily, and the Ryvita I had held was no more. One of the kites had dived on me and snatched it from my hand and it had at the same time taken a small nip out of my finger. Here also, Mum got bitten on her fore-finger by an insect and the bite came up in a blister that kept on growing. Eventually when the blister was about two inches long, the doctor had to lance it; and all the while we two boys looked on at the huge amount of fluid that drained out into the kidney bowl he was using.

At Naini Tal a retired missionary gave both of us a hymn book called *Golden Bells* and in it he marked a special hymn and requested that we memorise the first verse. I last saw *Golden Bells* about fifty years ago, so I cannot have cheated when I quote that verse I learnt when I was just six.

> It is a thing most wonderful,
> Almost too wonderful to be,
> That God's own Son should come from heaven,
> And die to save a child like me.

Once more I visited a school and was shown the classroom which I would be in when term started: it was not to be. Grandfather, the missionary in the Godavari district, had by now received a letter from Mother telling him of our escape from Malaya and our latest whereabouts and he was determined that we should come south to be nearer to him, where Mother would at least have some family support. He arranged a place for us two boys at Breeks School, Ootacamund (now named Udagamandalam) in the Nilgiri Hills of South India, where our own father, together with his brothers, had been to school a generation before. It was a boarding school with a Christian foundation. Somehow, against great odds, Grandfather using his influence had managed to persuade the powers-that-be to let us go south. As far as I know, no one else was allowed to transfer to another district of India.

Train journeys in India were lengthy affairs involving sleeping three or four nights on board and sometimes requiring two or three changes of train. This one was no exception, with the final change at Mettuppalaiyam onto a narrow gauge rack and pinion mountain railway which wound its way tortuously round numerous tight turns, as it gradually approached its destination at Ooty. The total journey length was some 1,400 miles from its starting point at Naini Tal. Ooty, the abbreviated form of Ootacamund, was at an altitude of seven thousand feet and had a very desirable English summer climate. Though you could have night frosts in winter, the sun would soon burn away any frost and the daytime temperature was always like a warm English spring day.

We did not have time to explore the new place. As soon as we were off the train, we went straight to the school and Harvey, at just five years old, and I, at six, were placed – literally – in the hands of Mr Fisher, predictably nicknamed Trouty. He had taught my father twenty one years earlier. As he now held on to us, Mother had to leave us, with Harvey kicking Mr Fisher as hard as he could on the shins and both of us crying our eyes out and I suspect Mother was also shedding a tear. We were now boarders in a strange school, in a new country, and it would be eight months before we would see her again when, at last, the long two months Christmas holidays would be due.

Mother had to return to the Godavari District to my grandparents' mission station on the plains, in the Telegu speaking area of India. She was to be a godsend to them as Grandmother was going blind and Mother was able to take over the household responsibilities and look after them both. They were then in their early sixties which, for Europeans working in the heat of India, was considered to be bordering on elderly.

6. Ootacamund

The commercial centre of Ooty had the unlikely name of Charing Cross and comprised a bazaar and shops and, further behind these, squalid rows of single story houses with an open sewer running down the centre of the muddy streets which separated them. This was definitely a no-go area. The school overlooked Charing Cross and on the one side there was a grass slope rising up the side of the hill to the main buildings of the school. These were terraced into the hillside so that the second floor, at the front, became the ground floor at the back. The building was pure red-brick St Pancras-Gothic with turrets and projections at every point. By far the largest room was the main assembly hall, two stories high and reaching up to the apex of the roof ridge, with ventilators and skylights at appropriate points high above. Beneath this was a sub-floor with the carpentry and general workshop. The carpentry master, whose domain this workshop was, had also taught my father back in 1922 and was one of the few Anglo-Indian teachers. At either end of the hall were classrooms, the administration office and the headmaster's office. Beyond the extreme left hand end, on a lower terrace, were the newer single story buildings holding the kindergarten and other infants' forms. One of my abiding memories of the kindergarten was the huge Mercator's projection of the world on an inside wall, with the British Empire, shaded red or pink, occupying a great proportion of the whole. They believed in indoctrinating us at a very early age. At the extreme right hand end and detached from the main school building, was the toilet block. This was in true Victorian public lavatory style with a separate 'Boys' and 'Girls' and necessitated, even in the monsoon, running or walking across the hard-packed and sun-baked clay playground to perform the necessary functions. The playground was a huge levelled area making up the rest of the terrace in front of the buildings.

Sloping diagonally up the hill in front of the school was a tarmacadam road with a continuous stream of traffic comprised mainly of well-laden bullock carts pulled by the patient, pale-cream, Brahmini bulls with a hump on the back. They were often yoked in pairs and the humps seemed to have been designed by the creator expressly for the purpose of nestling into the yoke of the cart. We watched this traffic with great interest, especially when the carter stopped to apply the brakes for the hill. This was achieved with a stick stuck through a loop of rope round the baulk of timber forming the brake and twisting the rope ever tighter. The baulk spanned across both wheels and the twisted rope pulled this hard against the iron bands of the wooden cartwheels. The accompanying tortured shriek when the cart got under way was appalling. With true Indian logic, the brakes were not only applied for going downhill, but also to go uphill and this despite the straining efforts of the poor beasts who were already overloaded. Looked at with lateral thinking this logic cannot be faulted. At least the cart would not run away backwards if the animals collapsed and somehow slipped their yoke: but I am not being fair. Today, looking back as a qualified engineer, I can see that these drivers were much more clever than I thought and their secret lay in the position of the timber log that served as the brake. When going uphill the timber log was behind the wheels and if the cart started to run away backwards, the weight of the log, coupled with rearward rotation of the wheels, would increase the tension on the rope holding the log and thus pull the brake on hard, bringing the cart to a stop. If the cart was moving steadily forward up the hill, however, the forward rotation of the wheels would release the rope tension and remove the braking effect so the bullocks were not in fact working any harder. The trick that I had missed as a boy was that the drivers must have changed the position of the braking timber from in front of the wheels when going downhill to behind the wheels when going uphill.

Ours was not the only school in Ooty. There was also St Hilda's girls' school and Lovedale School for the sons of the military, one of the chain of St Lawrence schools strung out across India. Breeks was the school for missionaries' sons; though it had just as many sons of teaplanters, civil servants and others. Now, in 1999, it fulfils the same roll for the sons of the Indian middle classes but still has a Christian based morning assembly despite its multifaith intake. Likewise, St Hilda's is completely Indianised; but I recently read a newspaper article, where a former pupil at St Hilda's in the late 1940s, on a return visit in 1996, found that nothing had changed: 'Little England', with an ethos that was British turn-of-the-century girls' boarding school complete with prefects and classes still conducted in English.

The boys' boarding house, Lushington Hall, and the school were both on different hills separated by three quarters of a mile, with the school playing fields halfway between on low ground with a stream running along one edge. The girls had a separate boarding house at Clifton Grange in a completely different location which I never visited and I have only a very vague idea of where it was. Both boys and girls went through from infants to nineteen and these older ones seemed hoary headed adults to us. Meals were in a dining room at the boarding house and this meant that we had to make the long trek between the school and Lushington Hall, the boarding house, four times a day: we must have been very fit. We were escorted in crocodile by one of the masters on a bicycle which had a Sturmey Archer three speed gear and I must have driven him mad asking him, on a dozen

Schoolboys in India, 1942, just before their sixth and seventh birthdays. Harvey left, with mother Iris (née Jumeaux) and Blake.

different occasions, how it made it easier for him to climb the steep drive to the Hall. I was too young to make sense of his patiently repeated explanation. The progress of our column could be followed by listening for the accompanying, rather monotonous sound of the repetitive marching song which we had been taught by some of the senior boys:

> Whistle while you work,
> Hitler bought a shirt,
> Mussolini wore it,
> Goering tore it,
> Whistle while you work.

We were issued, at six years old, with solar topees to keep off the harmful rays of the sun. These were made of pith for lightness, with a cloth covering, and because mine was particularly thick, about one and a half inches, I was thereafter nicknamed 'Bombproof'. What with these and khaki shorts and shirts, our crocodile must have looked like a miniature cohort of the British Raj. Perhaps it was this outfit that inspired the original for the caricature: the huge sun helmet, the comparatively large head, a skinny neck and the tapering of the body of a six year old as it ran down to a diminuendo at the feet.

The stream through the playing field was lined with the most beautiful arum lilies which grew in wild profusion. The stalks of these were fat, about half an inch in diameter, and pithy and we used to cut these into even lengths about nine inches long and tie them side by side with cotton to make rafts which were then floated down the stream. The banks of the stream were very muddy and we small boys playing there must have been in a terrible state but, being India, nobody seemed to mind. The soft alluvial mud of the playing field was also the home of enormous worms, similar to earthworms but probably of a different species; they were about two feet long and more and, like the millipede in Malaya, they were also about the thickness of a man's thumb. They were exposed when the groundsman stripped turf from the playing field or undertook any other digging operation. We collected these and kept them in a bed of dried earth in the small tin attaché cases which were part of our school equipment, together with any other wild life we could find. These included Bundu beetles, fat round iridescent jewels with brilliant blue or green wingcases; Johnny beetles, long, fast-moving, with formidable pincers that, placed across the earlobe of an unsuspecting victim, could extract maximum effect; stick insects; slow worms; and lizards. Of course, we had learnt that these could not all be kept in the case at the same time: even at that age we knew all about the food chain. Birds' eggs and butterflies were collected and the latter were humanely killed by placing them in a jam jar of crushed laurel leaves and then pinned out on a board for our collections. The birds' eggs, after they had been carefully pierced with a pin on the broader base and the contents sucked out, ended up in our attaché cases on cotton wool beds, when these were not being used by wildlife. This was a perfectly disgusting process, particularly if the eggs had become even slightly addled.

The playing field was used for football, hockey, netball and sports days and had a primitive corrugated iron pavilion with a raised veranda from which the smaller boys could watch matches over the heads of the older ones. The veranda roof was supported by tubular steel columns which we enjoyed shinning up and sliding down, leaving them in a high state of polish. The football first eleven was made up of boys of eighteen or so years old and we had our heroes, particularly the goalie, who was very good, and whom we saw most of, as the pavilion was just behind the goalposts. One of the casual helpers who sometimes refereed matches was a missionary called Fox. Why he was available for this and not somewhere on the mission field, I do not know; but he was full of energy and was always cracking jokes and had a fund of sarcastic humour, though he was never vicious with it, with the inevitable result that he became known as Brer Fox of Uncle Remus fame.

Of sports days I remember always coming in last in my races because I developed an exaggerated style, throwing out my arms and overstriding with my legs, using maximum effort to achieve minimum forward motion. I would pummel the calves of my legs before a race, in the way I had seen the older boys do to loosen up their muscles and this caused much amusement among the senior girls who had been put in charge of us infants. Egg and spoon races and sack races were a different matter. In these I excelled, having inherited my mother's finely developed sense of balance and coordination. She could walk across a muddy field with such dainty precision that not a speck of mud would mar her shoes. Later I was to find this talent very useful when I developed a passion for hill walking.

Lushington Hall was a large old colonial house, all single story, set in its own grounds on several acres of hillside with a winding drive through mature eucalyptus trees, some as much as one hundred and fifty feet high. It was the former home of one of the early pioneering administrators, C.M. Lushington, the brother of the Governor of Madras, who in the 1820s sited his house on this lovely hillside purchased from the Toda tribe. There were tennis courts, no longer used, set among the trees and, just in front of the house, there was a formal terraced garden with a large monkey puzzle tree from which we used to collect the milk coloured resin to make glue: terribly tenacious stuff that would not come off our hands no matter how much soap and water we used.

The house was built on two levels with the infants' dormitories on the higher level and the senior boys' dormitory and the dining room on the lower level. The construction was plastered brickwork with a cream lime wash and a columned entrance portico. Alongside the portico, we had been allocated a small flower bed and given some peanuts to plant as an exercise in nature study. It came as a surprise to us, when the plants had grown, to find that the peanuts were not on the bush, but were in casings attached to the root mat and had to be dug up. At the back of the Hall there were single story outbuildings housing the sick bay and various servants' rooms.

Adjoining one side of the grounds were the magnificent Government Gardens, more akin to botanical gardens, and home to several rare species of plant. On the other side it ran down to an open grassy valley at the head of which the Todas lived and beyond that were the jungle clad slopes leading up to Dodabetta, the highest peak in the Nilgiris at 8,760 feet.

The Todas were the indigenous hill tribe of the Nilgiris, as yet untouched by modern civilisation. They never washed, they were unshorn and the men wore nothing but a loin cloth. Their hair and beards were matted with clay. They were polyandrous, where one woman would have more than one husband and in many cases the husbands would all be brothers. They lived in semi-circular thatched huts with flat wooden or mud and wattle front and back ends.

If there were school rules, I never knew of them. There were no bounds and we were free to wander where we liked. I can remember walking in the jungle beyond where the Todas lived. It was wartime and our amusements had to be what we could make ourselves. We all had penknives or, if you were lucky, a sheath knife and with these we could achieve anything. We climbed trees to make tree houses and very elaborate some were. We would cut lesser branches to make the floor platform, lashed on to a suitable fork of the tree, and then the walls and roof would be constructed from finely interwoven branches. We used lighted candles in these tree huts and why we were not burned alive in the dry season, I do not know. Mind you, this was when we were a little older than the five and six years which we had been when we arrived.

We made catapults and peg-tops and gillidandus and we carved miniature models of Spitfires and Messerschmidts and entered mock aerial battles. Gillidandu was a game where you used a stick about two feet long as a bat with which to strike a stick on the ground like a three inch long double pointed pencil. If you hit it just right, that is on the point, it would spin up and you would then have to hit it again as far as you could while it was still spinning in the air. I do not remember how one scored but it was something to do with the distance the spinning stick travelled. The older teenage boys became very skilled in the use of catapults and were sufficiently adept to hit birds foolish enough to perch near them and many of them had extensive collections of the brilliantly coloured plumages of tropical birds. Peg-tops was another vicious game we played. We made our own tops with the heaviest, densest, wood we could find to form the body of the top, into which we then screwed a steel screw and filed its point needle sharp; and on this it spun. Round the cone shape of the top was wound a jathi, the cord from which it unwound when thrown. The game commenced with everyone slinging their top with a sweeping motion into a six foot circle on the hard packed ground so that it would land spinning within the circle and then either hop or spin out. If any came to rest within the circle, they would be pounded into the ground until just the tops were showing, and everyone would then aim at them with the intention of splitting them with the vicious spikes. But woe betide any top which then stopped within the circle, for it became the next victim. Some practitioners became so expert that they used techniques known as short sparks and long sparks. These made use of yo-yo throws to impart huge spin coupled with the necessary sideways motion to ensure their top hopped out of the circle. Short sparks was a below the shoulder throw and long sparks above the shoulder

Other seasonal enthusiasms were hopscotch, marbles and elaborate variations of leapfrog in which teams were pitted one against the other. Not only did we play the game of marbles, but the acquisition of these beautiful glass, steel or china baubles became its prime objective. Some of the glass ones had the most intricate of spiral patterns embedded within, others had a blend of plain sheets of colour folded inside the clear glass envelopes. The china ones would come in delicate pastels, some uniform in colour, some changing in intensity as one rotated the surface; with added lines and streaks to provide variety. There would be enormous marbles, known as dormies, usually between an inch and two inches in diameter. The dormies were prized, as their size advantage would knock any lesser marbles out of the game ring to enable the player to claim the one that had been knocked out. The most prized were the steel ones because of their enormous weight. These had probably started life as industrial ball-bearings. How the boys acquired them remains a mystery. Two variations of the game were played. One was a linear game in which the object was to roll your marble to hit that of your opponent, so that a hit would allow you to claim his. This game could extend as far as the playground allowed and the smaller marbles were preferred as presenting a lesser target. The other game was more suited to a number of players and was that mentioned above, where the dormies came into their own by knocking marbles out of a large diameter circle. It all depended on the season as to what the latest craze would be and the fun of it all was that no one could predict when and what it was that would trigger the next one off.

To emphasise the lack of school rules, I recall several barefist boxing bouts to settle quarrels amongst the older teenagers, with even us youngsters watching. These were held on the grass bank below the school grounds within partial view of the staff without any interference on their part. I think the prefects organised these to see that fair play was observed and I suppose the staff knew and accepted this. I have a clear memory of one of the boys, about fifteen, retiring after three rounds with his nose streaming with blood and a developing black eye. The girls of all ages would be watching but I was too young to know if any of these fights were over them. On one occasion, as I was leaving the toilets, a teenage boy burst in streaming blood from a self inflicted gash made while using a hatchet to lop off a tree branch. He was a popular boy with the girls and when he left the boys' toilet, after washing the wound under the tap and trying to stem the copious flow of blood with his handkerchief, he was immediately surrounded by a group of feminine sympathisers who tended his wound. There were no staff repercussions from this: they probably never knew.

Food in wartime India was limited to local produce but this in fact meant that we had the same healthy diet that our Indian neighbours ate. Not much meat, plenty of fruit, vegetables, cereals and pulses, of which lentils (dahl) and rice formed the bulk, some eggs, a little fish and poultry: an admirable low fat diet. What little meat we had was stringy, tough, full of gristle and tasted awful. It would be difficult to pin down which animal it came from.

Ootacamund

Most main meals were rice based. There were: curries, often vegetable or hard-boiled egg curries, sometimes chicken curries, accompanied by strange vegetables such as ladies fingers, a long thin green runner-bean like pod full of slimy pale cream balls – a distinctly acquired taste but delicious when mastered; pillaus with saffron rice; fish with plain rice; and stew with the unidentifiable meat and the inevitable potatoes. Tomatoes and potatoes, which grew in abundance, would have been the only recognisable English vegetables. The main course was followed by either fruit or a sweet of *peregu*, a sour yoghurt with a dollop of *jaghari* – the fine, soft, dark-brown, raw cane sugar or molasses that came in a loaf; or *ragi*, a semolina like cereal, again with or without *jaghari*. Peanuts also featured prominently in our diet.

Fruit was abundant. There were guavas, which were pear sized fruit; hill-guavas which grew on wild jungle trees and were gooseberry sized though matt green and, though not related, tasted like the cultivated guavas; mangoes; pomeloes, citrus fruit of about twice the size of a grapefruit but tasting like an insipid orange; limes; bananas; passion fruit; wild yellow raspberries etc. We particularly liked the yellow raspberries which tasted much like our English red ones and could be found anywhere, in season, growing on bushes with thorns just like our wild brambles. Many an expedition set off to find this bounty and that of the hill-guava tree.

Occasional illicit treats could be had from the *hulva* seller or from the *jelabie* stall if you had the necessary pocket money. These were forbidden for hygiene reasons. The *hulva* seller came surreptitiously to the dead ground of the bank just below the school playground and we made assignations with his rectangular wooden tray of cubes of jellylike sweetmeat with a similarity to Turkish Delight but without the sickly scented flavour of the latter. The tray hung from his neck by a leather strap. *Jellabies*, on the other hand, could only be obtained by a sneak visit to the strictly out-of-bounds bazaar, where these syrup-filled, saucer-sized squirls made up of hollow tubes of crisp batter could only be bought from the stall. They were quite the most delicious things I have ever tasted even to this day.

Another supplement to our diets were the occasional teas that accompanied invitations to the local missionary home, Montauban, which, from the front of the school, was half a mile down the road past Charing Cross; or we might be invited to the families of former missionaries who had retired to the hills. Our passport to these places was my missionary grandfather who was known to all these people. Montauban provided splendid spreads of English style afternoon teas of cakes, jellies, tarts and sandwiches, the like of which we had never seen at school, and the idea was that you helped yourself from a table piled with all these goodies. We certainly made huge inroads into all this beneficence: but then it only happened perhaps once a year and we had to make the best of this rare occurrence. One of my school friends was Colin Tilsley and we were often invited to his home where his missionary parents, then retired, would collect us in their great big black pre-war American limousine driven by an Indian *syce* or chauffeur. Colin had a much older sister Joy, aged perhaps twenty, and a teenage sister Heather, who patiently set us up with various toys and knick-knacks to play with; but we had one favourite, a stereoscopic slide viewer which magnified pairs of black and white 35mm slides. This instrument gave an incredible three dimensional view of whatever had been photographed and they had a vast and varied collection of these slides of which we never got tired.

Further along the road, which ran diagonally up the hill on which the school stood, was the Union Church where we younger ones went to Sunday School. My only memory of Sunday School was the folded paper that we cut out with scissors to unravel into a string of figures that might represent the disciples of Jesus or the Gaderene swine and so on, which we would then colour appropriately. Sometimes we would be given cut-out letters of the alphabet which we painted with watercolours and then had to paste onto a sheet of paper to form a biblical text.

A little higher still, and above the church, was a triangular open space formed by the junction of the roads where there was a group of shops, a club and tea rooms and the dentist. I hated the dentist and I am sure he hated me with good cause. I had heard so many dreadful things about his instruments of torture that, long before the drill came anywhere near my mouth, I was bawling at the top of my voice, which was unusually loud for one so young, and it must have given the impression to anyone in the waiting room that a murder was being committed. It was at the club tea rooms that I had my first strawberries and cream tea by kind courtesy of Major Morley, father of my best friend Michael Morley. Major Morley was serving in the wartime army in India and had come up on leave. Many soldiers were sent to Ooty for recuperation and rest and they were a great source of cigarette packets, cigarette cards and matchbox labels for our many collections which of course included stamp collections.

On the lower road between the school and Lushington there was a cinema. The whole school went to see 'Mrs Minniver', my first ever film, and one suitably patriotic and emotional at that stage of the war. It was well beyond the understanding of us little ones but I still thought it wonderful. The school took over the cinema to stage its end of term productions just before the Christmas break. As one of the best infant readers I was given a passage of the nativity story to read and can recall reading at a gabble, as fast as I could, under the impression that this was a competition in reading skills. This probably made the whole passage completely unintelligible to those listening. The more senior classes were given a French song to sing. The singing was so beautiful that I remember it now. It was the lilting melody of *'Sur le Pont d'Avignon'* and words that sounded to me like *'O-dondada, O-dondada, avec nez of O!'* repeated after each verse. I must find out what these words really were.

Opams and Bundu Beetles

At the end of the day, when we had all trooped back to Lushington and had had our evening meal, we prepared for bed. This was a civilised process with us infants sitting round, mesmerised by the flames of the log fire in Miss Bogey's room, listening to a bedtime story followed by a bible reading and prayers. It was often frosty at night in winter at that altitude and the fire was very necessary. Bed then followed with lights out. Miss Bogey seemed very old to our eyes but was probably on the right side of fifty. She must have retired soon afterwards because she was followed by a much younger missionary couple called Brimblecombe. Mr Brimblecombe was strict and we were a little afraid of him but his wife was a soft touch. The youngest of us were put to bed after lunch for a rest and there was much feigning of sleep when Mr Brimblecombe was on patrol. When he was gone we would get up to all sorts of activity to relieve the boredom. My bed was next to the wall and at mattress level, out of sight, there was a hole made by my predecessor in the soft plaster of the wall. My boredom relief came from gently rubbing the soft granular mortar with my finger to see how much bigger I could make the hole.

Preparation for bed meant cleaning one's teeth. There were no toothpaste tubes available in India because lead was given a priority for war use. We would clean our teeth by dipping our wet toothbrushes in a tin of Eucryl powder, much like a shoepolish tin, flat and circular, and then brushing our teeth with the damp powder. This was mildly abrasive, slightly salty and probably contained a mixture of salt and chalk, with a dehydrating agent to prevent it absorbing moisture. Sometimes we were given a round flat cake of Gibbs Dentifrice toothpaste, wrapped in cellophane radially pleated with a central circular sticker to hold the pleats. The cakes were refills, to be placed in the original tin, and one would rub the wetted toothbrush over the surface of the cake to give a slightly soapy textured slurry which was then applied to the teeth. Both methods seemed to be fairly effective.

Ootacamund

On half days off school, when we would be at Lushington we wandered the gardens and grounds and took up our various hobbies. Some half days were devoted to the barber who was generally loathed. He was a Tamil with a sadistic streak who had it in for the small British sahibs and he put to good use a pair of exceedingly blunt hair clippers with which he tugged rather than cut the hair. The other planned half day activity was bathtime. This was conducted on assembly line principles with queues of small boys in increasing states of undress the nearer they got to the baths and then they were processed by a team of Tamil women accompanied by great shrieks of laughter and much spilled water. The women enjoyed the whole thing as much as we did.

It was on one of these half days that I committed my first conscious sin. Corbett, a slightly older boy, the son of a missionary, had a paper bag with perhaps a dozen Smarties which he gave to me with the instruction that I was to have two and then distribute the remainder to specified friends. I ended up by giving one each to the specified friends and eating the remainder. Corbett was no fool and checked with his friends and I was caught red-handed. I was consumed with shame and even to this day I sometimes think about the betrayal of trust from a boy who had felt sorry for me. I had not been one of his friends but he knew of my circumstances and that I never had any treats.

Among other friends, all missionaries' children except for Michael Morley, the soldier's son mentioned earlier, there was Bramwell Booth, my classmate and rival for form marks, who was related to the founder of the Salvation Army movement; there were the two Bird brothers, one my form mate and the other two years older, both of whom I came across years later in England when my school played rugby against their school Kingswood, the well known Methodist College in Bath. There was Bostock, who looked the part, being strong and stocky with a round face and ruddy complexion and there was a boy called Veevers who had a thin face, gently receding towards the forehead, a thin nose and a generally streamlined appearance giving the impression that he could be useful in an athletics race. There were also several Americans who were probably children of missionaries. I cannot recall a single girl other than Heather Tilsley whom I only remember from visits to her home.

We all spent occasional periods in the sick bay with the usual childhood ailments or spells of quarantine. The sick bay had an airy open veranda onto which our beds were pushed. My main memory was the occasion when I was having my temperature taken and I clamped my jaw and accidentally bit the bulb off the end of the mercury thermometer. There was enormous consternation as Matron fished around my mouth to ensure that not a drop of mercury had escaped down my throat. She could not be sure and I had to remain under observation for some time. Alongside the sick bay was the maintenance workshop with a full time Indian carpenter who had a soft spot for Harvey. Harvey was very fair with light brown hair and blond sunbleached streaks, and he was not very robust, in contrast to later years when farming made him very strong. He was probably the youngest boy in the school at only five years old and everyone felt sorry for him. I, on the other hand, was robust, I was very dark, almost Anglo-Indian in looks, and I was also rather tubby. It was not surprising that the carpenter would make painted, wooden, model aeroplanes for him but refused to make me even one despite all my pleading. I considered this one of the great injustices in my life.

There was a small stationery shop run by an Indian clerk from a desk in the Bursar's office. You could buy pens, pencils, rubbers, paper etc. from it and the occasional more exotic item. One such was a small brass padlock and key which fascinated me. I could not have any feasible use for it, but have it I must. My mother had no source of income and my grandparents, as retired missionaries, were no better off, so there was no pocket money for the two of us. I managed somehow to persuade the clerk to let me have it on credit until my mother should next visit and then I promptly forgot all about the debt. I am sure that children of eight have no concept of this sort of obligation and it was months later, after more than one visit of my mother, that I was hauled before the headmaster, Mr Bury, in the presence of the clerk and had to return the lock. He seemed more annoyed with the Indian clerk for acting in such a naive way with so young a child. By then of course the novelty of turning the key and hearing the satisfactory click of the tumblers had long since worn off.

There were three lakes in Ooty. Ooty Lake, which was a large boating lake on which we once took a picnic with us on a hired rowing boat; Marlamund Lake, a reservoir of which I recall nothing; and Suicide Lake to which we went for nature study trips. Suicide Lake was surrounded by tall trees making it dark; but the water was clear and very deep with steeply shelving sides which enabled you to see right down into the depths. It had lots of water weed, which rumour said entangled any swimmer so that he would drown. The aquatic plants made it very suitable for nature study, with its many tadpoles, waterboatmen and other forms of pond life, but we were always a little afraid of this lake with its history of suicides and drownings. A cast iron water pipe disappeared into these depths, adding to the sinister atmosphere. We were always glad when we left it for the sunshine.

Harvey went into Kindergarten with Miss Chaves but, after a one week induction there, I was placed into Form 1, partly as a result of having been taught to read by Mother at home before we left Malaya. In one sense this was an advantage but it meant that I missed out on all craft work and the joys of messing about with paint that all children love, as these activities were confined to the Kindergarten. In Form 1 we were introduced to writing on slates that were issued to us and collected in at the end of the lesson. The accompanying screech of the scriber on the slate made one's blood curdle and any erasing was done by wiping over with a damp cloth. It was in Form 1 that we co-operatively made a model of the Toda encampment with its thatched mud and wattle huts.

The following year in Form 2, under Miss Snowden, we were given pens with steel or brass nibs but frustration was compounded in that we were not allowed to use them until the nibs had been immersed in water for twenty four hours. Why? – I have no idea. On the great day, powdered ink was mixed with water and carefully poured into our china inkwells in the right hand upper corner of each desk. We had been previously issued with lined exercise booklets in which sentences, in copperplate handwriting, had to be laboriously copied with all the letters being carefully formed to just touch the lines. The middle set of lines was used if one was writing small letters and the outer set of lines was used if the letters were capitals. Now you could have heard a pin drop as every head was bent over its work and the only sound was a steady scratching. Unfortunately the novelty did not survive the day and things were soon back to normal.

In Form 3 we began to do some slightly more sophisticated maths. It was in this form that we began to have regular tests and there was great competition to be in the first three, where one would be given a gold star for first, or a red and a blue star for second and third. My grandfather was very proud of the fact that I invariably got one of the coveted stars and so it was that he was shocked when my next report arrived with my position as bottom of the class. Why I did it I do not know, but I had deliberately faked the answers to give the wrong results. Who knows? Perhaps because of envious remarks from my not so fortunate classmates. Grandfather was unaware that it had been engineered and I got a very severe dressing down and did not dare tell him the truth. Even when later my mother told him the truth of what I had done, he was not amused. Form 3 was where we learned all our multiplication tables up to the sixteen times table because there were sixteen annas to the Indian rupee. We were even introduced to some simple algebra, which was very early for this sophistication but it stood me in good stead when, after the war, I went to school in England. In Form 4 we would have begun French but just as I was about to begin, events took over and our stay in India came to an end: but that comes later in my story.

7. Mission Station

That seemingly endless first school year, 1942, came at last to a conclusion with the coming of the Christmas holidays which, throughout India, was the main school holiday lasting a full two months. We now set off on the long journey to my grandparents' mission station in the Godavari district on the east side of India about halfway up the coast between Madras and Calcutta. The journey began with a four hour trip back down to Mettuppalaiyam on the same narrow gauge rack and pinion mountain railway that we had travelled on eight months earlier. It wound its way through deep valleys and river gorges, through tea plantations and then, at a lower altitude, through coffee plantations to finally emerge from the cool of the jungle clad hills to the searing heat of the open plains. On one side of the platform at Mettuppalaiyam the track was the two foot wide gauge of the mountain railway and on the other it was an enormous five feet wide. Indian railways in this part were not standard gauge. The change to broad gauge meant that an enormous amount of baggage had to be transferred. We all had a large metal cabin trunk, an attaché case and a bedding roll called a holdall: not a bit like the modern holdall. The bedding roll consisted of a large outer canvas, with full width pockets at each end, onto which was laid out a mattress made up with sheets, blankets and a pillow. The ends of this made up bed were then tucked into the pockets and the whole lot rolled up and tightly secured with straps for transit. It was given the name holdall because it had a multiplicity of smaller pockets into which you could put your toiletries, your light reading and other small possessions.

The new full size train fascinated us after the little train. It had windows that had several layers, all of which could be opened and closed in varying combinations and which became an immediate source of experimentation for us. There was the wire gauze flyscreen, like an English meatsafe before the days of fridges, there was the glass window, there was the slatted wooden venetian blind and there was the roller blind. There were switches which switched on and off various main lights and reading lamps, there were armrests which had to be pulled down and restored to position, there were upper bunks that lowered for sleeping, and at the very top, there was a netting rack into which you attempted to throw your smaller items for the journey. When you next wanted them it meant a bit of mountaineering to recover them. There was a door through to the toilet compartment which had a drop down washbasin with no drain outlet in the bowl but with a magical system of decanting the contents down a chute, straight onto the track, when the basin was returned to the vertical. This was also the case with the toilet when it was flushed and you could peer down its funnel to see the sleepers and ballast of the track hurtling past. There were all sorts of taps and plungers to be tried. Bedtime was simple; you drew down all the blinds, lowered the bunks, undid the straps and rolled out your bedding roll, switched off the lights and, if yours was the prized upper bunk, climbed up the ladder and got into bed. There was one dark blue light that remained on all the time giving a minimal amount of illumination for those who needed to navigate their way to the toilet compartment.

The train from Mettuppalaiyam was a local train and we had to transfer onto the express at Madras. It was at stations like Madras, the capital of the state of Tamil Nadu, that the true experience of travel in India was encountered. Madras, being a major station, was high ceilinged with many platforms covered with people sitting or sleeping or waiting for their connections. There were others buying food or drink from the many vendors serving piping hot meals from the various mobile stalls, there was a constant noise of steam being vented, engine whistles, guards' whistles, or calls from people selling wares. Cries of 'Lemonade, soda, tea, coffee, *garam pani*, cigarette, *beadie*, betel', would compete for custom. *Garam pani* was hot water used for washing and shaving, as the basins on the train would only be supplied with cold water. *Beadies* were the poor man's thin, hand-rolled cigarettes. Betel was a mild narcotic from the nut of the Areca palm mixed with a pinch of tobacco and a white powder of lime and wrapped in a betel leaf which, when chewed, turned strangely red and dribbled from the corner of the mouth. It was, unusually, favoured more by women than by men. Against all this hubbub, there was the rumble of yet another train rolling to a stop and the constant bustle of people getting on and off the trains. People would wander across the track with no apparent concern for their safety and often the hawkers would be trying to sell their goods from the trackside, climbing up on to the steps of the carriage and poking their heads through the windows; and all this activity continued throughout the twenty-four hours. Beyond the platforms were the crowded waiting rooms with the punkah wallah hypnotically pulling the cord to keep the *punkah*, a heavy, ceiling-hung curtain, running across the width of the room, slowly moving to stir the air and provide a gentle waft of breeze.

Here and there on railway stations throughout India were the occasional Sadhus in various states of undress. These were the Hindu holy men, and the most holy of these, often wearing just a loin cloth, with unkempt hair, bloodshot eyes and wild uncut beards, would have the whole of their bodies smeared in white ashes. There were others, considered to be not quite so holy, dressed in colourful robes with equally colourful face and body painting. But perhaps the most disturbing scene was the sight of beggars with a multiplicity of ailments. Many had open sores or ulcers; some had leprosy and would be missing a nose or part of a limb; others might have elephantiasis, a disease which left the limbs so swollen that a leg would look just like that of an elephant, often just one leg would be affected. There would be those with skin diseases showing a patchwork of patterns against their normal healthy dark brown to milk chocolate coloured flesh tones, with dead-white areas alternating against areas of angry pink inflamed skin. Amongst them there would be amputees on crutches; and polio victims propelling themselves on their hands, while their useless paralysed legs dragged behind; and then there were the professional frauds, the young man who would extract sympathy by turning his eyes right up into the sockets, so that only the whites of his eyes would show, and thereby feign blindness. Most beggars were the property of someone, often the family, who made the most of their potential earning power and, saddest of all, many of them were children. The station concourse was the ideal place for them to obtain the maximum exposure to the masses with the minimum need for mobility. India showed her tolerance in the way she accepted these poor people, where Western nations would have thrown them out.

When the guard blew his whistle, waved his green flag or, if it was night, raised his oil lantern aloft, the overloaded train imperceptibly gathered speed to great choughs and sighs of steam which gradually quickened to become a steady rhythmic beat. We would keep our noses glued to the windows until we finally ran out into the surrounding countryside of fields and villages which would pass by hour after hour at the majestic speed of 40 to 45 miles per hour, which was the speed of the express. The monotony would be relieved by stops at lesser stations where there might be a change of engines. The original locomotive needed to stock up with coal and water and, not least, the driver needed a relief.

Being wartime, there were many troops in transit on the trains and, at these smaller stations, the carriages would be beset by small boys and girls of our age, six to ten, singing, or doing cartwheels and handstands, or some other tricks with which to gain the soldiers' attention in the hope of being thrown some sweets or small coins. The smaller children were often naked. They learnt the popular English songs by rote, of which they could not understand a word, and would then sing them in the heavily accented and relatively tuneless singsong of all Asiatic music with its chromatic scales. It was hard even for us boys, with our attuned ears, to recognise the songs. I can remember only the first two lines of one which went:

> 'O! Johnny, O! Johnny, how I can louwe [love]:
> O! Johnny, O! Johnny, heavens' abouwe [above]'.

The letter 'V', in that part of India was pronounced as a 'W'. Presumably the man who taught them was reading from a book of popular songs. Another thing that surprised us was the way in which these children could walk on the sharp stones that formed the ballast of the track in bare feet. Their soles must have been like leather.

Very often at these lesser stations there were no facilities and the poorer Indians would perform their bodily functions along the track. It would all be quite decent as the long dohtis and saris they wore retained their modesty; but the smells would leave a lot to be desired. It was a relief when the train pulled out.

We finally neared our destination at Rajahmundry with the crossing of the river Godavari some 800 miles from its source in the Western Ghats, the chain of mountains that runs down the opposite side of India. At this point the river ran over a huge delta of shifting sand banks which, in the dry season, were fully exposed with just the one main channel taking the river flow. The bridge was over a mile long with pier after pier spanned by steel trusses and the train had to cross it at a rumbling crawl interspersed with resonating metallic echoes and clangs as each girder was passed. From here it was about forty miles by bus to the mission station at Koyyalagudem. On our return, however, the journey was initially by bus and then by canal because the timing of the express meant that we could not catch it at Rajahmundry north of the river but had to make the connection at Kovvur on the south side of the Godavari.

The buses were very old single-deckers with no window glass and were piled high with people, goods and livestock both inside and on the roof. The roads in these rural areas were hard-baked earth and lined on either side with large shade trees. The lime-washed houses in the villages through which we passed were made of wattle and daub weatherproofed with a smeared cowdung slurry which, strangely enough, smelt very pleasant when dry: reminiscent of hay. Later in the holiday, we would watch the women collect wet cowdung with their bare hands which they patted into cakes and then laid out to dry in the sun for fuel. People would also be mixing clay and chopped straw and placing this mixture in wooden moulds to form bricks. The countryside which we passed through was flat, as one would expect of the flood plain of the Godavari, and comprised mainly fields of crops, of which tobacco seemed plentiful. We sometimes passed tanks, the village ponds from which the villagers obtained their water supply. The long journey finally ended when we disembarked at Koyyalagudem.

Grandfather ran the mission with the help of Satayanundum, an Indian who had been one of his first converts soon after his arrival at Koyyalagudem, and Grandmother worked amongst the village women of the area. His task was primarily to travel within the district preaching the Gospel of Christ to the local peoples but, at the same time, and as a former schoolmaster, he would hold simple classes in the village to provide rudimentary education. Grandmother would bring the elements of domestic hygiene to the womenfolk and help them with their daily

Mission Station, Koyallagudem – Godavari District (mid-1930s).

problems. The mission was an outreach of the Plymouth Brethren and was entirely dependent on voluntary donations by members of this denomination. There was no salary and my grandparents had to rely on the random arrival of unknown gifts of money or kind. Visits home to England occurred on average once every ten years, when they were entirely reliant on the hospitality of the home church members and they were expected to tour England and conduct a gruelling schedule of lectures about their work. These lectures would help to raise the funds for the continuation of their mission.

The mission station was completely cut off from the outside world and they were always several days behind with the news of the major events which were occurring at that time. There was no electricity anywhere in the rural areas and the radios of that time, with the high current demand of thermionic valves, could not be run off batteries and even the post would have to be collected from the nearest town several miles away.

My grandparents' home was a two storey, stone house with a

tiled roof, purpose-built in the early thirties to my grandfather's own design, with a scattering of outhouses in a fairly large compound in which the buffaloes were kept when they were not grazing in the surrounding scrub grassland or on the road verges. The walls of the house were not constructed with the neatly dressed stone associated with houses in England but were formed from large plums of roughly trimmed sandstone bedded in thick layers of mortar.

There was a well in the compound down which we loved to drop stones to watch the water shimmer some fifty feet below and we also used every excuse to lower the bucket and watch it drop with a plop and then we would tug the rope to tilt the bucket so that it sank. We were too small at nearly six and nearly seven to haul it up. The domestic needs, and the thirsty buffaloes, were dependant on this water supply. In the house the water was poured from buckets into large earthenware pitchers with damp muslin covers where the slow evaporation of the water as it seeped from the porous pots and muslin covers kept the whole thing cool. The buffalo milk could not be allowed to seep and was stored in a cool pantry in brass bowls with dampened cloth covers: there were no fridges in those days. The cleaning of these brass pots, and the iron pots and pans used for cooking, was done by the women using water and sand to scour them and they were then left in the sun to dry.

The house perimeter walls had no windows and were made up of open stone arches on both floors. The overhang of the roof and first floor formed a balustraded veranda on both levels so that you could walk all round the house and enter any room from the veranda through the appropriate arch. This meant that the house was shaded on every side and that any breeze there was could blow right through it: a very necessary requirement in the extreme heat of the plains. The arches had slatted wooden shutters in lieu of windows, like the houses in Mediterranean France. I remember flower beds surrounding the house with

Eustace Blake Bromley and Anna Elizabeth (née Herwig), my missionary grandparents.

mainly bougainvillaea plants which thrived in the dry conditions and a few small tired shrubs which did not, presumably because there was insufficient water for them. Once we found a snake in the grounds, a krait, sheltering in the shade of one of these shrubs and the gardener came and killed it with one of Grandpa's walking sticks. We also found some rubbery snake's eggs under a bush and these would have presumably been destroyed. Lizards, crows, kites, vultures and many other birds, beetles and scorpions seemed to be the only other wildlife in the area. We never actually encountered a scorpion but were told to keep a lookout for them, particularly in our shoes.

Grandfather's roots were from the south of England and he had trained as a schoolmaster but in 1903 his widowed mother, he and his sister heard the call to the mission field and sailed for India. Grandmother came from central Germany but she had, from a very early age, always wanted to be a missionary. They had first met when their paths crossed in the Godavari but they

Mission Station

only saw each other on rare occasions, being separated by many miles of river delta. Addressing each other by surname only, they began a courtship by correspondence and 'Crossing the Rubicon', as he puts it in his diary, he proposed to her after a few months. Her return letter arrived six days later and on 20 January 1907, his diary entry makes this wonderful understatement, 'Went to the Post Office where I received Miss Herwig's answer. To my great joy it was to find that Elsa is mine.' This was the first time that he had used her christian name. Her father was a shoemaker and her grandfather had been the bandmaster in the small university city of Kassel. Her German nationality meant that she was confined to the Godavari mission field area during the First World War, where the prolonged period in the intense heat of the dry season seriously damaged her health. But by the Second World War, a more enlightened attitude allowed her freedom to travel to the cool of the hills during the hot season.

We went for walks with Grandpa in the surrounding flat and somewhat monotonous landscape, where we sometimes saw the village buffaloes, which were attended by a diminutive herdsman, perhaps eight years old, using a switch to move them on as they grazed. The buffaloes were impervious to this puny beating and would not be hurried. We liked nothing better than to accompany them and to watch them wallow in the local watercourse.

On 17 January 1943 I had my seventh birthday and Grandpa gave me a book that he was given on his seventh birthday in 1889, inscribed by his father with his dates, and now he had repeated the inscription for me with my dates. The book was *Masterman Ready* by Charles Marryat and had navy-blue hardbacked covers with pages that had yellowed with age and these pages had a few silver fish holes through them. I treasured that book as well as enjoying the Victorian tale of the sea and I think it was the only possession I ever had from this grandfather who, as a missionary, never had enough money and equally had no access to shops. I gave that same book with a third similar inscription to my own son on his seventh birthday in 1970.

Apart from seeing Grandpa go off on his bike or on the bus on some preaching assignment and Granny teaching the women in one of the outhouses, I do not remember much more about our one and only visit to the plains as, soon after that, the health of both my grandparents began to deteriorate and they started the prolonged process that led to their leaving the mission station for the more healthy climate of the hills. Grandmother's blindness was later confirmed as glaucoma but she was sent to Madras where the specialist made the wrong diagnosis and operated on her for cataract. She had two more corrective operations without success and went through a great deal of unnecessary pain. Mother accompanied Granny as she was sent back and forth for her operations as, during this time, Grandfather had developed a heart condition. At the end of all this fruitless journeying the decision was made for the three of them to move up to Coonoor, the next major town ten miles east of Ooty down the line of the narrow gauge railway. Grandpa had now officially retired after some forty years in the missionfield.

8. Coonoor

The move to Coonoor was a great blessing to Mother as she was now close enough to see us for even the shortest of school holidays, when a simple train or bus journey took us the ten miles home. Simple it may have been but certainly the bus journeys were anything but pleasant, what with the steeply winding roads and those early 1930s petrol engined buses with very little power. There were no such things as diesel buses with their high torque engines and so it meant that the engine would whine away in an excruciating scream of high revs, which might have been tolerable if the noise had remained constant; but the twisting road and ever changing gradient meant that the crescendo of noise from the double declutched gear changes was overwhelming. I was a poor traveller and would be nauseous all through the journey and Mother would sometimes have to ask the driver to stop the bus so that I could get out and be sick.

For the first two years in Coonoor, Mother and my grandparents went to live in Arnside, one of two small bungalows owned by Lady Ogle. The other bungalow, in which she lived, was called Silverdale, both named after towns from the English Lake District across from Morecambe Bay. Lady Ogle was an aristocrat with a strong Christian faith and extended her charity to those missionaries who, after a lifetime's service, had no pension for their old age. Arnside came fully furnished with typical colonial Indian furniture including a pair of two foot high, black, carved elephants; brass ornaments; a table with an intricately worked brass top about three feet in diameter and an embossed brass gong. We loved to bang this gong, which resonated satisfactorily for several moments after it had been hit with the felt covered striker, to announce that meals were ready. Grandpa, being relatively immobile now, had two great passions in this home. The first was chess, and he would try to persuade anyone and everyone to give him a game, and the second was doing jigsaw puzzles: the more complicated the better. He had one which was handmade, cut from plywood with a fretsaw, that occupied three quarters of the dining table when complete and lasted for at least three holidays before we saw the finished product. The dining table could not be used during this time and I imagine we ate at a makeshift table in the kitchen. The subject was the battle of Trafalgar and all the pieces seemed to be either sea, sky or rigging. We used to enjoy finding all the unusual shaped pieces that one gets with handcut jigsaws: pieces that looked like a sword or an old-fashioned backdoor key or a cat. I do not think we contributed much to the progress of the puzzle.

Granny was a compulsive letter writer and being so isolated while in the missionfield, her large number of correspondents were her lifeline. Now, because of her blindness, this had all come to a stop and Mother, knowing how important this was to her morale, made several efforts to help her to write, including attempts to provide a frame with string stretched across the writing paper to provide a guide for her pen, but these all proved abortive: the string line sagged too much. Mother knew that if she could get a typewriter, then perhaps she could teach her to touch type, a skill that Mum had not forgotten from her secretarial days; but of course this was wartime and typewriters could not be had. My grandparents and Mother believed in the efficacy of prayer and made the hoped for typewriter a regular item in their daily devotions and, in the course of time, the expected miracle happened. Apparently someone who had sent in their typewriter to the local repair shop for a complete overhaul never returned to collect it. Perhaps they died; but, whatever the reason, Granny got her typewriter and every successive holiday at Arnside we would hear the slow but steady beat of the typewriter keys imperceptibly getting faster as she gradually mastered the machine, and her isolation from her many pen-friends was finally brought to an end. From the time that she went fully blind, Granny was also never without her knitting and she was the source of many pullovers and pairs of socks for the family.

Not far across the road from the house was Tiger Hill cemetery where we visited John's grave. John only lived to be seven weeks old and was my father's youngest brother born in 1924, fifteen and a half years after Father, long after Granny had thought she had finished having any more children. He was a healthy good sized boy but succumbed in just two days to debilitating tropical diarrhoea. On the far side of the cemetery was the Anglican church, only one step removed from the heresy of the Roman Catholic church, according to my nonconformist grandparents, and under no circumstances were we allowed to enter in case we were contaminated by their doctrines. I wonder what they would think if they were to know that for several years I was treasurer of our local Anglican church and Harvey was churchwarden at his Anglican church for several years and that we have very good relations with our neighbouring Roman Catholic church?

At the end of the drive to the two cottages was a wrought iron gate commanding the entrance to Hebron, the girls' boarding school which was considered to be the sister school to ours, and where Father's sisters had gone in the 1920s. If you continued walking well beyond the cemetery and down the hill you came to the station and the bazaar area. Our favourite stall in the bazaar was that of the goldsmith. We sat for a long time watching him blowing with his bellows to heat the miniature furnace on which had been placed a small crucible inside which were the chopped up fragments of mother's gold ring. She had slipped and had sat awkwardly on her hand with the fourth finger twisted back and this had resulted in the inevitable break. The ring had had to be cut off and her finger never returned to its original size. We saw the gold begin to soften and then quite suddenly it coalesced into a liquid pool. The molten gold was poured into a mould which the goldsmith split open, and the ring that emerged from this was dropped into a bucket of water to be handed to Mum, to try for size, before it received its final polish. Every finishing operation on the ring was carried out over a piece of felt to ensure that not a single filing of gold was lost.

My mother walked everywhere and was extremely fit and, despite her small stature, went on many a long walk with friends of her own age to explore the surrounding countryside. They walked into the hills where they would be in jungle for some distance and then they might emerge onto a tea plantation or find themselves along a river in a ravine. In one such place when we were present, we found tiger's pug marks in the damp soil; though it would not have been dangerous at the height of the day unless we had actually stumbled on the tiger where it lay up. Some way from Coonoor was a precipice called the Droog, which had a sheer drop of a thousand feet, over which Tippoo Sultan, at the time of his mutiny against the British in the early 1800s, drove captured English soldiers to crash on the rocks below. Mother's greatest achievement was to walk the thirty two mile return trip to the Droog, setting off at dawn and arriving back at dusk and though we could never have walked this far, she did once take us to a lesser jungle clad precipice which looked down over the plains. The sense of awe and vertigo was compelling and I could well relate to the fear and despair of those soldiers as they looked out over the abyss.

Mother took us on a trip by bus to Kotagiri, a small village about ten miles away, reputed to have the most agreeable weather in the whole of India and consequently it was the setting for some beautiful homes for retired expatriates. I remember those lovely homes and the broad beaten-earth road along which we walked through the village and the tingling sense of fear of wild animals as we walked further along it into the dense jungle beyond. This part of the Nilgiris, the name means 'Blue Hills', was as yet undeveloped and the possibility of encountering wild animals was not unlikely and certainly their tracks were often seen by us. Mother was on a pilgrimage to Kotagiri because her uncle, Dr George Leach, had lived here before the family moved to Malaya. It was here that his daughter Sybil died in a tragic accident and one of Mother's half sisters had been named after her. The little girl, probably between two or three years old, was going to have a bath. There was no mains water and she would have had to bathe in a galvanised iron tub filled with boiling water to which cold water would be added. When the Ayah, the Indian nanny, or perhaps the *rungima*, the sweeper or cleaning lady, went out of the bathroom to fetch the cold water, Sybil climbed straight into the bathtub and, by the time the household responded to her screams, it was too late and the little girl died of her terrible injuries. There would have been no hospital within less than a day's travel. Mum was very sensitive and I am sure she shed a tear or two for her cousin on that pilgrimage.

The school cub pack went camping near Coonoor in a glade in the jungle through which a stream ran with a boulder strewn waterfall at its upstream end. The only thing I can remember about it was swimming naked in the plunge pool with all the excited shouts and squeals of delight from this group of small boys. We had never been allowed before to take off all our clothes. Unfortunately, Harvey and I had to return early from the camp and miss all the rest of the fun because Mother had booked Harvey in for a minor operation.

It was about this time that I became aware that I was different from most of the other boys in that I was circumcised and they were not. In those days it was the fashion for many non-conformist families to have the boys circumcised in obedience to

Old Testament teaching. It was also thought to be a good hygiene measure in the tropics; but how could one sustain the logic of this argument when the greater part of the world lives in these climates without the benefit of human reshaping and suffers no ill effect? I had been circumcised as a baby and have always resented this mutilation in which I had no say and from which there is no return. My wife told me that Mother had made great stress to her, when our son was a baby, of the desirability of having him circumcised. Needless to say, this advice was not taken.

Another minor cause for curiosity, now that I am talking of medical matters, was the very large vaccination scar on my arm. I was told that I was vaccinated as a baby by a semi-blind doctor. In those days, a hollow cylinder with a sharp circumferential edge, about the diameter of a pencil, was used to cut a neat cylindrical ring on your arm into which the smallpox serum was wiped. This doctor's eyesight was so bad that he could not see whether he had been successful on the first attempt and so he tried and tried again. I have four separate ring markings that have overlapped each other to form this massive pockmarked scar.

On our second Christmas holiday, this time in Coonoor, we were taken to a puppet show in a hall with a raised stage on which a miniature Punch and Judy style theatre was positioned. The play was called 'Once in a Blue Moon' and the stage lighting created a wonderfully romantic atmosphere, with everywhere dark but for this silver moon set against an indigo background, and the true fairytale princess with long blond tresses picked out in the foreground. I do not remember the storyline but the moon did turn blue in the end. The experience was magical. We were taken to another play in this same theatre which had a title something like 'The Monkey's Paw'. It had a macabre final act in which this detached shrivelled monkey's hand, with no supporting arm, takes on a life of its own and jumps from where it was lying on the table, to clutch the throat of the villain in a vice-like grip and strangle him. I had great difficulty in going to sleep for several days after that.

My grandparents gradually needed more care than Mother could give unaided and so the three of them moved to Wyoming, the YWCA home in Coonoor, which had resident staff and a dining room where meals were provided. Mother had a large room with an en-suite bathroom and an external fire escape on the first floor and Granny and Grandpa had a room on the ground floor where they had access to the public rooms and would not have to climb stairs. The move proved a good one for Mother, as the hostel was primarily for women and there were a number of ladies of her own age with whom she made friends after her previously rather lonely existence. One of these friends had a portable wind up gramophone which used 78 r.p.m. records and this lady was trusting enough to lend it to us when we were back from school: a great act of faith. We loved the routines of winding it up, changing the metal or thorn needle every two or three records, moving the arm across, releasing the turntable brake and lowering it onto the record. In our clumsiness, we inevitably caused scores across the record as we knocked the needle arm to the accompaniment of a great screech. The records were songs like Jeanette MacDonald and Nelson Eddy's 'Rose-marie, I love you...'; a few songs from Gracie Fields and Vera Lynn; and a sprinkling of classics.

From the high vantage point of Mother's bathroom fire escape we could watch what was happening at the back of the house. This was the servants' domain and therefore much more interesting. The hens, ducks, a goose and two or three turkeys were kept here and I remember the first goose egg we were given to eat. It had a very rich, deep-yellow yolk and was big enough to make a meal for all of us. Around Christmas, from the door exiting from her toilet onto the fire escape, we watched the Indian cook and his helpers chase each turkey in turn and, with a sharp knife, cut off its head. With blood pumping from its neck, the dismembered body would continue to run around and flap for a short while until with no controlling messages from the brain and the lack of blood to the muscles, it would collapse in a heap and its involuntary spasms would gradually die away. This was a horrifying sight for us but Mother did not know what we had been watching, thinking that we were just using the toilet, and we never told her. On another occasion, while in this lookout, we watched yet another snake being killed by one of the servants.

My second encounter with a bike occurred here. It was borrowed and was full size, much too big for me, and this time I had no servant to wheel me around. I was convinced that I had learnt to ride in Malaya and so I set off boldly down the YWCA drive. I achieved two successful runs but I had no idea how to get off at the end of each run and more or less fell off. The second time I put out my hand to break the fall and promptly sprained my wrist. That was the end of further experimentation with riding a bike.

9. The End of the War

The later years of the war at Ooty were interspersed with special days, the memories of which would stay with us for the rest of our lives. 'D-Day', 'VE-Day' and 'VJ-Day', each one bringing hope into our lives that perhaps we would one day see Dad again. There was no guarantee that this would be so as, throughout the nearly four years that he was in Japanese hands, Mother only received three pre-printed postcards of the 'I am well/I am not well – *delete where applicable*', variety and these had no indication of where he was or what he was doing. When he eventually returned, we learned that he had been working on the notorious 'Death Railway', the railway from Thailand to Burma which the Japanese had built for the invasion of India and, when that had been completed, he had been shipped to Japan to work in the factories near Osaka. His particular factory was a steel rolling mill producing the steel sheet and other rolled steel items for the Japanese war effort. He has mentioned to me incidents of how the prisoners attempted to sabotage, in an undetectable manner, the products of this factory. In Osaka he was subjected to Allied bombing raids in just the same way as the local population and eventually the prisoners were transferred to a remote spot, which the bombers were unlikely to target, on the northwest coast of Honshu island at its closest point to Korea. Here the POWs were made to unload by hand cargoes of manganese ore being shipped from Korea. It was very hard work indeed.

En route to Japan Father had been shipwrecked on Taiwan,

Formosa as it was then called, after the Japanese skipper had deliberately driven the ship ashore when it was foundering after three days being tossed about in a typhoon. While on the ship, before it was wrecked, the prisoners were kept battened down in the holds and Father had to undergo an operation without anaesthetic to extract a rotten molar on which the dentist could get no purchase. It eventually had to be chiselled out and he remained in agony for several days.

As soon as the D-Day news was known, the whole school was assembled in the main hall for the announcement and for prayers for those who had gone on to the Normandy beaches that day. This was followed by cheers for the success of the first landings and, immediately the noise had died down, a lone young voice piped up and said, 'And three cheers for the prisoners-of-war because my Daddy was taken prisoner by the Japanese.' Though that young voice was mine, the whole school took up the spirit of the occasion and gave out a resounding three cheers, much to the amusement of the older ones.

At another morning assembly, not long after D-Day, prayers were said for one of the senior boys who had run away from school and was gravely ill in hospital with a fractured skull. He had taken one of the masters' bicycles without permission and ridden down the road which descended towards the coastal plain on the western side of the Western Ghats, of which the Nilgiris are part. This road was noted for being very steep with numerous hairpin bends and sheer drops as it wound its way through the jungle clad hills and it was at the foot of one of these drops that he was found unconscious by a passing motorist. The assembly prayers must have been answered because, after a week or so of being in a coma, he eventually regained consciousness and over many more weeks made a slow recovery. Apparently the bike had gained more and more momentum despite his applying the brakes full on and finally he had lost all control and went over the edge.

The End of the War

VE-Day was the cause for great celebration and not only did we have a free day from school but on the golf course, after dark, there was a big bonfire with a fireworks display attended by the whole European community. Small knots of boys wandered up to the golf course during the afternoon, a place at which we would not have been welcome in the normal course of events, and so we were thus unaware of the object or conventions of the game which we now observed with interest. When two balls landed near us with a plop, Harvey, who had always been good at throwing, thought that he was being helpful when he threw the two balls back to the approaching players. One minute we had been absorbed spectators and the next we were being chased off the course to the accompaniment of lurid words that had not appeared in our vocabulary before. None of this however spoilt the enjoyment of the fireworks in the evening, way past our normal bedtime, as we melted into the anonymity of the dark. VJ-Day saw similar celebrations but I find it hard to separate what exactly we did do on each of these occasions and the golf incident could have occurred on either one of them.

After all the excitement, we had reverted back to the routines of everyday school life, so it came as a complete surprise when two months later, returning for lunch to Lushington, I was called out of our usual crocodile formation and was told to cross the road and enter the school playing field unescorted. As I entered through the gate, I could see in the distance, two figures standing side by side waving at me, so I assumed that was why I had been diverted and set off towards them. I had not gone far when I recognised Mother and then, incredibly, I recognised my father, whose face I had not been able to conjure up in my mind until that moment when, after nearly four years' absence, the reality brought his features flooding back. He was in a smart new soldier's uniform. I must have run faster than I had ever done in those earlier sports days, shouting 'Daddy! Daddy!', and threw myself into his arms. We all hugged each other for a very long time. The moment was so intense that I cannot remember if Harvey was there before me or had arrived later, but that long, long day was one of intense family joy and privacy. I believe we went at some stage to Montauban for a celebratory tea and it may also have been on this occasion that we went boating on Ooty Lake.

Father looked thin and his face was gaunt, but his happiness and Mother's overrode all the past deprivations and sorrow and for the next month, until term ended, the two of them lived in Mother's rooms in the YWCA and had their second honeymoon; while we continued on at school. It must also have been a great joy for my grandparents, in their old age, to have their son with them after all their years of sacrifice when, as missionaries, they were separated from the rest of their family.

Father had been released from the prison camp in Japan by the Americans some three weeks after the war ended. During those three weeks the prisoners had lived in limbo, the Japanese guards having melted away on the day the surrender was announced by their Emperor. The prisoners were unsure of the attitude of the surrounding, recently defeated, civilian population but they clearly had other things on their minds and left the prisoners alone; and some of the prisoners had even ventured out into the countryside to try to obtain a little food. They soon found that the local peasantry were even worse off than themselves in that the prisoners had been fed, albeit at starvation level, whereas the Japanese government had left the rural population to fend for themselves and had at the same time commandeered whatever crops they had. The pathos of the starving children soon had the prisoners giving them small items of food from the rations that the Americans were parachuting in to supply the prison camp for those three weeks before release. It was the state of these children more than anything else that removed from my father any bitterness that seems to have lingered over several decades with many other POWs.

The End of the War

Because Father, unlike the rest of the prisoners who returned to England, wanted to be sent to India to rejoin us, his journey became a series of short hops over a period of weeks until he eventually arrived at his destination. All the prisoners were initially taken from Japan to Manila in the Philippines where they were placed in a transit camp for recuperation and rehabilitation. The Americans showed extreme generosity and kindness to the POWs and built them up physically before they were allowed to leave: my father was twelve stone in weight when he was taken prisoner and was six stone when released. He was eventually put on a transport to India. Only the Americans would have had sufficient confidence in their unit commanders, and the captains of their ships enough self-belief, to show the initiative that enabled my father to hitch-hike right across the Far East in this informal manner: and we owe a great deal to them.

10. Deolali

School term having ended and the Christmas holidays being with us, no time was wasted in trying to obtain passage back to England. The British authorities had now acknowledged Father's presence in India and arranged for the family to be taken by train to the huge military depot at Deolali, situated about one hundred miles northeast of Bombay. Once again, it was a long train journey, but this time we had the whole sleeping compartment to ourselves as a family. As officially part of the army, the fares were paid for and food was issued in the form of American 'K' rations. These were prepacked waxed boxes with all the essential foodstuffs for one person's needs for a day and consisted of items like processed cheese, tinned sausage, Spam, biscuits, wrapped butter portions, jam and various sweet items including chocolate: something we had not seen in years. Never having eaten Western foods, this was very special and we boys could hardly restrain ourselves from breaking into the next day's ration.

This journey was different on two counts. The first was that we crossed a desert somewhere on the route and we saw several bleached skeletons of large herbivores and the occasional carcass being recycled by the crowds of vultures tearing at it. These would be seen through the train windows, at first as tiny dispersed dots circling high above us in the sky and then they would materialise at some object at the trackside, hopping in that malevolent sideways gait with their scrawny necks doubled up

Deolali

beneath the bald head that looks to be all curved beak. They frightened us with their sinister looks and movements and their greedy squabbles, constantly fighting amongst themselves to tear out the choicest morsels; and all this would be accompanied by the sickly-sweet smell of death. The people of the desert were different too. We were familiar with the intense black faces and round eyes of the Dravidian races of the tropical south. These desert dwellers were taller with the longer faces and the keen, slightly screwed up eyes of the northern races that had invaded India and their skin was much fairer. Their clothing tended to be the looser Indian dhotis that modern educated Indians favour rather than the borrowed Western clothes of the south.

At Bombay we experienced the second of the two counts in which the journey was different. We changed on to an electric train and a dual track of modern construction. This train had tremendous power and could hurtle up the slopes of the Western Ghats at an estimated fifty miles an hour and on the flat it must have been doing sixty, according to Father who had timed the passing of telegraph posts with the sweep second-hand of his pocket watch. Then the train coasted the long downward run, with brakes gently applied, until it reached the scorching plains surrounding Deolali. We spent much of the time with our heads out of the windows without any fear of getting coal smuts in our eyes. Fortunately, being a hot country, this probably did not do our eyes too much damage, as would have been the case if we had done this on an English train in the biting cold.

Deolali Depot was a vast encampment of barrack hutments with supporting office buildings, canteens, workshops and all the other infrastructure you would expect of one of the major military bases in India. There was a large parade ground and the whole area, which was flat, was brown and sere with grass clearly struggling to survive: in contrast to the green jungle clad hills from which we had come. I imagine the monsoon would change all this. We were given one of the huts to ourselves and were left to our own devices with only the need to comply with routine at mealtimes, when we would make our way to the canteen. This was a self-service cafeteria serving English food such as bacon and eggs, sausages, corned beef, tinned tomatoes: all foods that we had never encountered before and therefore delicious, despite the fact that they were not nearly so healthy as the indigenous foods we were used to. Most of the rest of the time was spent in going out as a family for walks, or best of all, going on the organised swimming parties.

We had to travel in army buses, about fifteen miles on dusty dirt roads, for our swim in the lake. It was not a beautifully clear lake with aquatic plants in nature's balance, but a large, water-filled depression in a flat barren landscape, with barren hills rising just beyond. I imagine this lake was on a clay stratum and was topped up each monsoon season and was of sufficient capacity to avoid drying up in the hot season. The edge of the lake sloped down gently to form a beach and about thirty yards out there was a duckboarded diving platform kept afloat with oil drums. The coolness of the water was a great relief from the heat and we were soon fooling around and splashing with shouts and screams as all children do in water. At some stage in the games, because of the shelving bottom, I found myself out of my depth and only some five or six yards from the diving platform; so I set off with tremendous efforts of a wildly splashing overarm stroke to reach it and I eventually made it to the loops of rope that hung around its perimeter. I do not think that I was in any great danger because Dad was not far away, but the result of all this was that I had learnt to swim, even if it was not in a very elegant style, and Father subsequently encouraged me to try several more times until my confidence had developed. We went on these swimming parties on a number of occasions during the rest of our stay in Deolali.

There were itinerant tradesmen passing through the cantonment and one of these was the barber; so Dad made use of the opportunity to have us all made smart for the coming voyage to England. The barber cut our hair next to a paddock where he had set up the chair that he took around with him and, while I was having my hair cut, Harvey had discovered a donkey foal and its mother in the paddock. He had always had an affinity with animals and he could make them do things that I could not. One presumes that the donkey mother was tethered, because Harvey was able to persuade the foal to come to the paddock rails without interference from the mare, and he then used the rails to climb on to its back and sit there quietly. His passion for animals was so strong that, from very early on, he had determined that he would become a farmer; and that is exactly what he did very successfully through all his adult life, despite having no background in that profession. When I saw Harvey on the foal, I shouted to him, 'Don't let him go, Harv!' and waited for the barber to finish so that I could have my turn. Harvey then went across to the barber for his haircut, while I climbed up and sat myself on the foal. Harvey was slight, I was much bigger and heavier and it is no wonder that the poor foal should suddenly tip me off and run bellowing his indignation to his mother. She replied in great neighs of 'Eyore! Eyore!' as they trotted off to the furthest extremity of the paddock.

Christmas must have passed at Deolali but I do not remember a thing about it. Now as I look back on it, I do not remember receiving any presents the whole time we were in India, other than the *Masterman Ready* book from my grandfather, and, apart from the end of year school carols and the Christmas dinner at the YWCA, I do not recall any Christmas festivities at home and I do not think we ever celebrated our birthdays. Mum never had any money and often there were no shops, and where there were, there was very little available and in any case there was nothing in the way of toys. I do not think that we were even aware that we were missing anything: that was the way things were in wartime and I have never felt any resentment about it. In many ways our lives were much more fulfilled, with the freedoms we had, than all the pleasure that any number of gifts could have given us.

Shortly after New Year's Day 1946 and just one week before my tenth birthday, we boarded that same electric train and journeyed straight to the docks in Bombay to embark on the *Strathnaver*, one of the P&O passenger liners of some 20,000 tons. We waved a final 'Goodbye' as the ship sailed for England and the last thing that we saw, slowly disappearing over the horizon, was the dome of the Taj Mahal hotel and the adjacent diminishing arch of the 'Gateway of India'.

Part 2

POSTWAR ENGLAND THROUGH THE EYES OF A YOUNG BOY

ENGLAND
(1946-1949)

11. Sailing Home

Sailing home: if ever there was a misnomer it was this. Every Englishman living in India thought of England as being home but for us this was a meaningless concept. Our imaginations could not project images of a country that we had never known; and the austerities of war meant that we had not even seen the picture magazines that we now take for granted, with their twee images of half timbered cottages covered in snow. And yet this is what we were sailing towards as repetitive day succeeded repetitive day.

There were many families like ours, with fathers from the armed services, all being returned at His Majesty's expense, and the endless days at sea, though repetitive, were fun for us children on board *Strathnaver*. Ships' hulls in those days were not designed to the exacting hydrodynamic shapes that the enormous power of modern computers allow and their designs were largely intuitive, followed by scale model testing in large rectangular water tanks. It was these very imperfections of design that made it such fun, because our ship ploughed its way through the water, not in the streamlined manner of modern ships but in great swirls and vortices and with huge bow waves followed by numerous smaller secondary waves. During that first week, my tenth birthday came and, equally quickly, it went. There was just no landmark to make it any different from any other day and I have no recollection of it.

The water of the Indian Ocean with its indigo skies above was almost black in colour and because of the heat of those latitudes, the top half of the boarding entry ports in the ship's sides would be opened to allow a draught to fan throughout the length of the ship. We would spend hours leaning right out of this port, like a stable door, watching the swirls and the trapped miriad of miniature air bubbles trying to break out of them. We would watch the change in colour from indigo to royal blue where the reflected light bounced off the bubble layer until we would get giddy from the constant backwards and forwards movement of our heads trying to keep pace with the forward motion of the ship, as we watched the successive patches of foam pass along the boat's side. We would study the turmoil caused by the intersection of the bow wave with the parallel lines of the pervading swell; we would look for that extra big wave from way ahead that would send a huge cloud of spray to wet our heads as the ship butted its bow into the next roller. The combinations were endless and this, coupled with looking over the stern rails of the ship, with the turbulence of the boiling and churned up wake to watch, would keep us occupied for hours.

Other amusements in the warmth and sunshine of the equable self induced breeze on deck were provided by the many open-air games of quoits, badminton, hopscotch, hoopla and so on and, while our parents were either reading or sleeping in the canvas deckchairs, we would be tearing around in endless laps of the upper decks, or chasing each other into the passageways and up and down the companionways of the ship. *Strathnaver* was a large ship of the 1930s and gave plenty of scope for the release of our energies. Despite this, the ship's officers must have felt the need to channel some of these energies into organised activities if only to give the longsuffering parents some time of peace and quiet. There would be supervised games, quizzes and storytimes, the occasional children's party and, memorably, the pancake eating competition which I won and now look back on with dubious horror. I think I ate eight pancakes.

Sailing Home

The Indian Ocean was left behind with our passing the island of Socotra and the Horn of Africa and moving into the shallower, incredibly clear, turquoise waters as we entered Aden at the entrance to the Red Sea. The ship anchored here to take on water and to re-provision and we were treated to the sight of very young children, no more than ten years old, dressed in the skimpiest of loin cloths, diving from the dockside for the coppers that the ship's passengers threw overboard. We would watch the coins see-sawing downwards as they rapidly began to disappear into the crystal depths; and then the dive of slim, young, naked bodies descending like an arrow after the coins and breaking into a stroke of minimum effort in their practised ease, as they caught the coins and tucked them into their loin cloths; and their much greater urgency as they swam up to break surface in great gasps. Their reward would have been no more than a few annas or pice in Indian money and they would have lost most of this to the middle men in the currency exchange.

Aden, though very hot, was paradise compared with the stifling conditions we now experienced in the Red Sea as we travelled up towards the Suez Canal. The Red Sea is enclosed by barren mountains of red-brown rock which reflect the sun at the ship and one is never out of sight of this enclosing, forbidding land. At night every porthole and hatch was open and one slept as near naked as was decent in those inhibited days and even then sleep was almost impossible in the heat. The huge deck scoops that funnelled air from the ship's forward movement became useless as they only served to discharge air that might as well have come from a hair dryer. In the daytime, it was only a little better on deck where awnings had been rigged and, in consequence, the intake of cool drinks went up by huge amounts. No one, including the children, had any energy to do anything except to crash out in the deck chairs. So it was that the approach to Suez came as a great relief.

A gathering of ships was marshalled into convoy at the mouth of the Suez Canal and we entered it, passing through partly in daylight and partly at night. It was a strange experience to be moving steadily forward on a ship through a desert landscape with occasional palm trees and then to see a string of camels sedately walking towards the ship, as they used the line of the canal as a navigational aid. Halfway through the canal we came to anchor in the Bitter Lakes to enable an outgoing convey to pass before we resumed our journey and, as we neared the end, civilisation gradually encroached. More and more villages and cultivated fields appeared, and then suddenly we were entering Port Said and, because we had travelled the latter half through the night, it came as a great shock to find, when we woke up and went on deck, that it was bitterly cold and that we had to put on our sweaters. It was winter in the Mediterranean!

The Red Cross had organised a party for the children of the ship in an empty dockside warehouse. The ship was anchored well out in the harbour and our attendance at the party involved a long trip in an open launch which, on the outward journey in the evening sunshine, was an exciting adventure as the boat threaded its way through the crowded harbour full of the flotsam of anchored ships and smaller vessels which, now that the war was over, had no further purpose. Though exciting, as we threaded through the multiple reflections of the ships' riding lights and those of the fixed lights alongside the docks, the return journey became almost unbearable because of the intense cold. This was aggravated by the wind chill factor created by our own forward progress; and this despite the fact that we had all been issued by the Red Cross with thick, grey and brown, herringbone-patterned, tweed overcoats at the party. To someone from England, it probably would not have felt particularly cold, but to us, just one day from the furnace heat of the Red Sea, it seemed like Siberia.

The Mediterranean Sea was yet again a different blue from those of the Red Sea and the Indian Ocean: a shade somewhere between the two. The changing colours seemed to result from a combination of the sky colour and the depth of the water. The deeper the water, the darker it became, but the lighter more northerly skies would superimpose to give ranges in between, so that the Atlantic on a fine day in the Bay of Biscay would look an almost royal blue, while the adjacent English Channel looked green. Etna, snow covered with its classic cone and the highest volcano in Europe, left a lasting impression as we swept between Malta and Sicily and I next saw it, with a strong sense of déjà-vu, when I went out with the Royal Navy some years later to Malta. We finally exited the Mediterranean into the bottle green shallower coastal waters of Spain beyond, as we passed through the Straits of Gibraltar, with the towering silhouette of the white-grey Rock at their entrance, and the African mainland appearing as a low silhouette on our left and then receding, as we processed onwards.

The ship passed within sight of Cape St Vincent on the southwest corner of Portugal and sailed northwards, often with the coast in sight, until it rounded the northwest point of Spain and headed through the Bay of Biscay on a direct course for the English Channel where, in the pitch blackness just before our bedtime, Father showed us the lights of the Lizard, the first fragment of the Cornish mainland that we could see and the first glimpse of England: albeit just some pinpoints of light against the inky background. The ship then went on through the night to round the Isle of Wight and enter the Solent.

Next morning, Father woke us up early and had us dressed and on deck in our new overcoats just after sunrise at around 7.30 a.m. on a still, frosty morning as the ship proceeded with slow dignity up the Solent. With our thin, unacclimatised blood, we were frozen; but the impact of our first view of the towns of Shanklin, Sandown, Ryde and then Cowes, was so stunning that we forgot all about the cold in our absorption. Nobody who is familiar with England can appreciate how beautiful it is, unless perhaps they are returning after years abroad. The Isle of Wight was a gem, with rolling, green, frost covered hills and those incredibly neat and tidy towns of red-brick houses and their contrasting darker tiled roofs, set in rows with vertical columns of smoke rising upwards from their chimneys into the static air. Interspersed were larger manor houses and parklands and those tidy, hedge enclosed, green fields; all set against the beautiful silver ribbon of the brimming Solent at high tide, with just a hint of mist above the water, soon to be burnt off by the steadily rising sun.

The fussy steam tugs caught their prey in Southampton Water and, seemingly reluctantly, the large grey ocean liner was hauled into its berth in good company amongst one of the much larger red-funnelled, black and white Cunard Atlantic *Queens* and the similar sized, lilac coloured, Union Castle liners that plied the South African run. Main engines were stopped and, apart from the hum of a generator or two, the continuous rumble that had accompanied us all the way was now no more, only to be replaced by the dockyard noise of cranes and stevedores and opened holds and the shouts from the shore. This was England: this was to be our new home.

12. First Impressions

Everything seemed neat, everything seemed tidy and everything was done with quiet understated efficiency as we disembarked through the customs formalities onto the harbour rail terminus; with porters trundling baggage that had just been lifted from the depths of the ship's hold to spin first one way and then the other, as it was suspended on pallets from great heights by the giant dockside cranes; and to then swing down in a giant arc as it was swiftly lowered to the ground, with last minute braking by the winchman that left you thinking everything would smash to unidentifiable pieces. We had stood on a high vantage point on the upper decks looking down with fascination into the cavernous depths of the many tiered holds, now swarming with dockyard labourers, as the unloading progressed. The noises came from the machinery, not the men, who seemed to work from a pattern of handsignals that could not be drowned by the constant bangs and whines and screeches of the processes that were slowly disembowelling the ship. Now we were out on the railway platform, about to board our train, watching a porter driving a three wheeled Lister diesel tug, its single cylinder engine thumping away to diminishing echoes as it approached the guard's van towing strings of flatbed trolleys loaded with luggage from the ship.

The waiting express train was very clean and was headed by a Merchant Navy class steam locomotive, streamlined and looking squat and powerful, with wheels that were not spoked but had the surplus weight of metal removed by radial lines of holes of increasing diameter drilled out of them: a most unusual effect that gave it an ultra modern look. The locomotive and carriages were painted in the green livery of the Southern Railway Company. The whole train seemed to be much smaller than those that we had been used to and, though this was actually so, the effect was also enhanced by the illusion created by the high station platforms which were absent in India, where you would have been looking up at the train from at or near ground level. The uniformed station staff all seemed purposeful and increased the sense of a well run and well ordered country: a far cry from the apparent chaos of the platforms of a major Indian railway station.

The inside of the railway carriage was another surprise. Instead of the individual compartments of our Indian trains, the coaches had a narrow corridor which gave access to each compartment and the small toilets at their ends, and each coach was linked to its neighbour by a flexible connecting corridor. All this gave great scope for exploration and venting of surplus energy and, running down its length, somewhere towards the end of the train, one came to a restaurant car. If you went in the opposite direction, you would stumble on a guard's van with a secure cage for valuable items and pigeon holes for letters and, somewhere within, a guard. The guard could be of uncertain temperament depending on whether he liked children or not.

The journey required one change to the local line and then a short bus ride to 15 Brockhurst Road, my aunt and uncle's home in Gosport: the town across the mouth of Portsmouth harbour. Gosport was a naval town and we were to see a great deal of shipping in what was to become our new home for the next nine years.

Uncle Wilfred was in his middle fifties and, sometime after his first wife had died, he had married my father's sister Millie who was twenty one years younger than him. The older two children of his first family had left home and were married with children of their own and only Joy, now eighteen and engaged to a hostilities-only sailor in the Fleet Air Arm, and herself a Wren, lived at home with the two children of the second marriage: David, four and Esther, two. Uncle and Auntie were now to include Harvey and me in their family from the time when Mother and Father were to leave us to return to Malaya at the end of Father's extended leave.

We had never before seen anything like this house at which we arrived on this our first day in England. It was a substantial house, if you qualified that in terms of elevation: a town house of the mid 1800s in a terrace of what, when new, were probably the homes of middle class professionals and middle ranking naval officers. But it had by now seen its best days and was beginning to look a little run down. It had five floors plus an attic for the maids' bedrooms and a cellar, all one room wide, two rooms deep front to rear, with a staircase and half landings all the way up from which the rooms were entered directly: you could say the staircase was a vertical corridor! The front rooms were always a half landing higher than the back ones. Thus you went up a flight of steps from the road to the entrance hall landing, off which the sitting room at the front of the building was accessed. Directly below the sitting room was the cellar which was conveniently placed for deliveries of coal or other household provisions to be offloaded through a trapdoor-covered shoot at road level and then, if you went down from the entrance hall towards the back of the house, the half landing led you into the kitchen at ground level with access to the back garden. A similar half landing upwards from the entrance hall led to the dining room and so on up the house. This meant that meals from the kitchen had to be rushed up two half flights of stairs to the dining room. The next floor front was the bathroom and thereafter, alternating back and front, were the bedrooms.

One finally reached the cold attic where, in more affluent days, the unfortunate servants slept.

The original open coal fires in the bedrooms on the lower floors had been converted to gas, and electricity had been installed up the house as far as the master bedroom and guest room, but above that the house was lit with gas lamps. We two boys considered ourselves lucky because we were to sleep in one of the upper rooms. It was much more fun to watch Uncle crack open the gas tap until a gentle hiss could be heard and then strike a match and light the gas mantle, which glowed dully until he thought that it had sufficiently warmed up to turn the gas full on. The mantle, made of chemically treated woven cloth, would instantly turn a brilliant white, giving off a substantial amount of heat as it let out a soothing hiss that would soon lull us to sleep. We were not allowed to light the gas lamps because these mantles were so fragile that if one just touched them, however slightly, they would disintegrate into a fine powder that showered down onto the floor. Gas also worked the geyser in the bathroom, which was a large, water-filled, copper cylinder strategically placed over the bath, with a permanently lit, blue-burning, pilot light. When the hot tap was turned on, there was a great whoosh and the whole of the burner at the bottom of the cylinder would ignite to heat the water now flowing through the cylinder. Regulation of the temperature would be controlled by the bath tap which governed the rate of flow of water through the apparatus. The slower the flow, the hotter the stream of water from the tap. This, and many other wonders, we had never met before.

We only stayed two nights in Gosport as the school term was already in its third week and we had been on holiday since the beginning of December. Because Dad would eventually be going back to his original job in Malaya, he had arranged for us to go to a boys' private boarding school called Eversfield, in Solihull, in the West Midlands and then, in the holidays, we would stay

First Impressions

with Uncle Wilfred and Auntie Millie or with one of our other relations or with close friends of the family. Eversfield was a Preparatory School taking boys from the age of six to thirteen and preparing them for the Common Entrance examination for the Public Schools which were to take them on to School Certificate and Higher Certificate and then on to University Entrance at the age of eighteen or nineteen. Most Preparatory schools were linked with one or two particular Public Schools, though this was not sacrosanct and one could go on to any Public School from there. Eversfield was linked to Monkton Combe School, both schools having a strong evangelical Christian tradition and it was for this reason that Father had chosen them.

In one frantic day we scoured the Portsmouth shops for the bare essentials needed for school. The bus journeys took us through the city centre and we were appalled at the bomb damage. Whole blocks of weed grown rubble piles interspersed with the gaunt silhouettes of twisted steel girders, with the occasional mementoes of what had once been there. A bath still hanging two stories up only held above the void by its plumbing; the remnants of someone's wallpaper on the only remaining façade, in a room that was once lived in and was no longer there. We had not experienced any devastation like this in India. Further contrasts were the grand municipal buildings, the trolley buses and trams with their overhead cables and the solid substantial shops of the city. We had only experienced the small towns of rural India, lacking these facilities, and had never ventured beyond the railway stations of those few cities we had passed through. But despite all these differences, the greatest impression was in the pace of life. In India people ambled: in England they walked with purpose as they hurried to their destination and it was almost certainly as a result of the two opposing temperature extremes of both countries. Who would want to walk fast in a temperature hovering round 100 degrees, and would one not want to generate some internal warmth by brisk exercise when the surroundings were near freezing? Perhaps the whole ethos and approach to life of any country is governed largely by factors which are external.

The following day, a green double-decker bus took us to the Gosport ferry. The double ting of the bell as the conductor sent the bus on its way, and the sudden acceleration had us clinging desperately to the handrail as we fought our way up the spiral staircase to the prized upper deck front seats with their Olympian forward view. We had only known the antiquated single-deckers of India, too crowded to see very much more than a small part of an obstructed side window. Though for safety reasons the conductor sent the bus on its way, when it came to getting off, we had the satisfaction of pulling the leather cord that ran along the length of the bus to the bell, to make the loud ting that informed the driver that we wanted to alight.

The Gosport ferry was a flotilla of small steam boats, about the size of the smallest tugboats, which ran a shuttle service at ten minute intervals across Portsmouth harbour. The landing jetties on each side of the harbour had floating stages which accommodated the very high range of the tides and the ferries would approach these at great speed then, at the last moment, the engine-room telegraph would clang, the engines would be thrown into reverse and the seemingly inevitable crash would become the gentlest of nudges, as the ferry came alongside the stage. Two crew would swing off at bow and stern and even before they had secured the ferry, passengers would be jumping off. It was all incredibly efficient and absolutely no time would be wasted in the disembarkation and subsequent boarding. Once embarked, you had the choice of standing on the always crowded deck, just three feet above the water level, or going into the smoky lounge below deck, with its view of the water streaming past just six inches below the porthole.

From the ferry one had wonderful views of all the shipping

in Portsmouth harbour which, at that time, included five battleships, one of which was *Vanguard*, the flagship of the British Navy.

Right by the ferry on the Portsmouth side was the Portsmouth Harbour railway terminus at which trains from Waterloo disgorged their passengers for the Isle of Wight. Along one arm of the station was the Isle of Wight ferry, which was a middle sized paddle steamer, one of many named after the towns of the island, *Ryde, Shanklin, Ventnor* etc.

Our little family of four boarded the train for Waterloo, a Southern Railway green, third-rail, electric train which was all just boring carriages, the electric motors being slung under the coaches. Once the train started, it was different. The acceleration of the electric train was tremendous and we seemed to fly along, at first through the city, and then through those wonderfully green fields of England. To eyes accustomed to the drab, sere-brown fields of India, England looked all emerald.

When we got out at Waterloo, the station seemed enormous with its vaulted roof spanning into the distance. We caught the tube for Paddington, another new experience, and boarded the train for Birmingham and school. The train now was a GWR express in its chocolate and cream livery, with a handsome green King or Castle class steam locomotive heading it, with polished brass funnel ring, nameplate and safety valve cover. This journey, after the electric train, seemed to go on for ever and was very slow; perhaps because by now we were getting very tired with the excitement of all the new things we were experiencing, each of which needed savouring and cataloguing in our memories. We finally reached our destination at Birmingham to the sound of a very strange accent announcing *'Sno Eel, Buurmingum; Sno Eel, Buurmingum – all chinge.'* (Snow Hill, Birmingham)

The local train onto which we transferred was pulled by an engine with rectangular water tanks either side of its boiler which made it resemble a matchbox and hence the name by which it was known to us schoolboys – 'The Matchbox Tank'. The carriages were what now comprise slam door trains; that is a hinged door to each compartment, opening outwards onto the platform, and no connection between them. This train stopped at perhaps six or seven stations before it pulled into Solihull where we got off. If, as happened later, we had left the express at Warwick and had got the local train to Solihull, it would have stopped at a station *en route* called Hatton. Hatton had a mental asylum and we schoolboys would all peer with curiosity out of the train windows, to look at what we thought were the lunatics on the platform who were, no doubt, unsuspecting local businessmen or housewives, about to take the train into town to go to the office or to do their weekly shopping. From the station it was about a mile walk to the school passing through Solihull town centre.

13. The Headmaster

The school was a red-brick, late Victorian or Edwardian house of considerable size set behind a tall holly hedge, with three floors and attic bedrooms above and with the usual large bays and other turret-like projections that houses of that era had. The front garden was small and consisted of nothing more than tarmac on which the headmaster's car and those of visitors would park and in one corner of which would be piled huge mounds of coke for the central heating boilers. Grafted at right angles onto the main house and running back from the road on the extreme left, was a new block with a flat roof, purpose designed for school activities, comprising: on the ground floor, an assembly room which, with folding concertina wooden screens, could be transformed into two separate classrooms; and on the floor above, two modern dormitories. The flat roof above was asphalted and was surrounded with iron railings so that we could go onto it via a small flight of stairs during our breaks. Just in front of this building was what were probably garages now converted into lavatories. On the extreme right of the frontage was the headmaster's suite, a newer extension to the house, with his study, his lounge, his bedroom and a guest room. The original building housed the kitchen and further classrooms on the ground floor and the main bathroom, dining room, staffroom, sickroom and yet more classrooms on the first floor, with the matron's room, library, music room and more dormitories above and in the attic spaces. The attic dormitories would get incredibly hot in summer and were very cold in winter.

Behind all the main buildings were the original gardens with a huge mature cypress tree centrally placed in a formal lawn and this lawn was edged with other mature shrubs. On the left side of the garden was a substantial wooden hut which was our hobbies room. Beyond the garden was an asphalted playground and further back were various huts before you came to the school playing fields with the headmaster's fruit and vegetable garden. These huts comprised the carpentry shop; a bicycle shed; the pavilion, which also served as a gymnasium; a workshop for the handyman and the groundsman; and finally, a shed that held the lawnmowers and roller for the cricket pitch, the wall of which had a secondary use as the cricket scoreboard.

Our arrival was greeted by the headmaster. It was not every day that colonials arrived mid-term and he had somehow to fit us into the curriculum, and for this, it was necessary for us to have assessment tests: which is precisely what we were set in the half hour following our introductory tour of the school. These tests determined which classes we would be in in any particular subject the next day, when work would start in earnest. We were now boarders confined to the school premises until the end of term and we had to say our reluctant goodbyes to Mother and Father. It had been a whirlwind start to our new life in England.

Our new headmaster was a sandy-haired man in his fifties with a severe centre parting and slicked down, rather thin hair and ginger moustache, who wore a tweed sports jacket and clerical dog collar which made him look the no-nonsense disciplinarian that he was; but he was not an unkind man and was always strictly fair even when wielding the cane or slipper. He had several hobbies which he shared with the boys and which made him seem much more human to us even though we would never have dared to cross him and, with hindsight, I now appreciate what a good educationalist he was. He engaged our interest in everything he did and made of us enthusiasts.

Cycling was one of his enthusiasms and on Sundays, provided that the weather was reasonable, the whole school would cycle to the beautiful village church at Barston, some six miles away, so that we could attend the Anglican service conducted by his friend of the cloth. You can imagine this motley collection of boys of eight to thirteen years old, cycling in a peleton like the Tour de France – only, in this case, they were travelling at a snail's pace, being herded or, for those who had dropped off the pace, being rounded up by a master who would encourage them to catch up. Fortunately, in that first year after the war, there was little or no traffic on the country lanes which have probably long since been swallowed up by suburbia. And then the whole trek would have to return and a tired group of boys would sit down to Sunday lunch. The boredom of the church service would be relieved by observing the gyrations of the thread like worms that would be illuminated by sunbeams shining through the water of the glass flower vases that were placed strategically on the window sills or by the buzzing of the occasional bee that managed to enter the church and fly around pollinating, in a lost cause, those flowers that were never destined to procreate.

The enthusiasm for cycling would extend to other expeditions into the country on half days which would on occasion range to fifteen miles: not bad for such youngsters and we were all very fit. We were taught the skills of cycling by riding round the playground and we learnt how to do violent controlled skids by jamming on the back brake on the cinder tracks at either end of the playground. This was achieved by locking the front handlebars to one side and by sticking a leg right out to pivot around our well worn shoe leather. We soon mastered the technique and no longer fell off: a good grounding for future speedway stars but I hate to think what this did to the tyres at that time of scarcity. The staff encouraged us to learn the technical side of stripping a bike down or repairing punctures until we became quite proficient and we made good use of these skills in later years. Of course, the smaller boys could not ride on the roads and they would be taken on expeditions in the headmaster's 1930s Daimler with its open body, canvas pramhood roof and celluloid windows which had to be placed in position and secured by press studs. This car had a semi-automatic pre-selector gear with a lever on the steering column with which you could select the next gear well in advance of needing it, and only when you subsequently depressed the clutch would the gear change. When we posed the question, 'Please Sir, how does that work?' we got the mysterious answer, 'It works through a fluid flywheel,' which left us none the wiser.

Because our parents belonged to the Plymouth Brethren denomination, Harvey and I were unfortunate in that arrangements had been made for a married master, Mr Coleman, who was also of that denomination, to take us to the Brethren meeting in the town centre and so we missed the Sunday cycle ride. We did occasionally go to Barston when Mr Coleman was away for some reason and we loved those summer runs.

Sunday was always our favourite day because not only was there no school, but the cycle ride, and a particularly nice set of meals in austerity rationed Britain, was followed in the evening by a special magic lantern show in the crammed headmaster's annexe. Sometimes, when as at half term, most of the boys had gone home and there were only those of us whose parents were abroad, these shows would be held in the headmaster's sitting room. This would be more correctly described as a snug with comfortable leather armchairs and generally male club furnishings; but for our Sundays, these would be pushed back to make way for rows of seats which would just about accommodate the boarders left behind. The magic lantern was an old Victorian mahogany and brass one with two projection lenses so that separate images could be made to blend on the screen and it took large three inch square glass slides. We would sit in excited anticipation as we waited for the show to begin.

Mr Peacock seemed to have an unlimited collection of slides packed in sets that made up a story, or a slightly saucy sequence of humorous anecdotes, some of the *de rigueur*, Black Sambo variety, or a biblical parable; and some of these slides would be animated. Animation would be achieved by superimposing onto a fixed glass slide, a rotating or a sliding glass, within what must have been a very expensive frame, which had gearing or cams to provide the requisite movement. Coupled to this was the ability to project the two sets of images together from the upper and lower lenses. One animated slide I can remember was of a monkey eating a banana and scratching his head, all at the same time. These slides were hand painted and would nowadays be worth a fortune.

Saturday evenings sometimes followed the same pattern for a number of us. Selected on a strictly fair rotation, the chosen few would all troop up to the head's study; but this time it was to play with his electric '00'-gauge train set. The head was a bachelor and loved his boys in a collective and wholesome way: no sexual innuendo or connotations as might now be the case. He was a typical bachelor man's man of the Edwardian type and his pleasure was in seeing the development of our curiosity and eagerness for life. His miniature train set was permanently set up on a table top which could be lifted off to clear the room and consisted of oval loops with various crossover points and sidings. The rolling stock was comprehensive and he had many fine engines, some with tiny working headlamps lighting the way, and he had coaches and goods wagons, together with some foreign sets. One which I particularly liked was an early Swiss electric locomotive with an overhead pantograph and its set of matching carriages. The whole layout was equipped with stations, signal boxes, fields with scale model animals and tractors and a tunnel into which the train disappeared and from which we would expectantly await its reappearance.

We would never be allowed to operate the speed controller but once everything was set and ready to run, by special favour, we would sometimes be allowed to operate the points. This was fine if you were on the set of points where the track diverged and whatever way you set the points the train would take one of two alternatives but, if you were on the points at the other end of the loop, which way did you set them so that the approaching train did not derail? I was very unpopular because I could never work it out and would have last minute changes of mind, which would set the train into spectacular derailments despite his shouted warning to leave it as it was. I was soon debarred.

During the dark evenings of the winter months after prep, we would descend to the hobbies room. This was equipped with a table tennis table and a number of other leisure activity features, the most outstanding of which was, once again, a model railway layout. But this time it was an 'O'-gauge and it seemed very big, set on seven-ply boards laid on trestles and occupying one third of the hut. The track was three-rail electric and the headmaster had at least a dozen magnificent locos, some old, like the 'City of Truro' class GWR engine that was the first to exceed 100 miles per hour, and some more recent ones, including 'Castles' and 'The Royal Scot'. Most of his locos were clockwork with two pull-push levers projecting from the cab: one to stop the mechanism, the other to reverse the motion. Their scale meant that they were superb in detail and the coaches, some Pullman, were outstanding. Many had working equipment and the electric ones had their interiors lit by miniature bulbs. I am sure Mr Peacock had never really grown up and was happy to have us as his excuse for playing with his trains at every possible opportunity.

That first term went by in a blur as we tried to integrate into this new and alien world. We had not done any French or Latin and I must have been two years behind and had to attend special classes, for we were not the only ones who needed to catch up. With regard to the 3Rs, we were, if anything, ahead of the others. Our History had centred on the development of colonial India and the British Raj, from the days of the original Dravidian Hindu India and through to the Mogul invasions that brought the divisions of race and religion, with their Muslim influence, that led to the later partition of the country. We were experts on this and could draw very creditable detailed maps of India and its provinces, we knew all about Clive and Plassey, but we knew nothing about English History or Geography. Thus began my first introduction to the Tudors and English History. It seemed that the Tudors were the favourite of all History masters as we always began again with them whenever there was a change of master or school. I never did learn much more about other periods of English history until after my schooling had finished.

Boys from India developed what was known disparagingly as a 'Chi-Chi' accent, a sing-song intonation that you still hear from English speaking Indians today. It took at least two terms before we lost the accent and this so irritated one of the school helpers, an elderly widow by the name of Mrs Lee, who had an extreme Yorkshire accent, that we fell foul of each other. Her duties were to shepherd us to various places of assembly; to oversee our meals; to supervise our bathtimes and our preparations for bed, which latter was preceded by prayers kneeling at the foot of our beds. She often used to leave her dentures out and this gave emphasis to her pendulous cheeks, and she had the habit of repeating over and over again, in her strong Yorkshire brogue, the same phrases, which came out somewhat slurred as a result of this habit. Her favourite was 'Give over! give over! give over! give over!' This soon became a murmured incantation by groups of boys, conducted in a stage whisper, whenever she approached them.

When the bell had rung for the end of a class, there would be a rush for the toilets. These had washbasins and changing facilities, with pegs for hanging clothes and benches beneath at one end, and a long urinal against the wall at the other end. In the rush to relieve oneself at the urinals, a competition would develop as to who could project the highest jet up the height of the urinal wall: no prostate problems with these youngsters and, in the inevitable excitement, voices would get raised to a higher pitch, as the contenders vied with each other as to who had achieved the ultimate. At the height of all this Mrs Lee rushed in, grabbed me and pulled me out of the toilets. She thought the high pitched voice was my sing-song and that I was the ringleader of all this discreditable activity. I had been a fascinated but innocent bystander and had never experienced anything like this in India. She was absolutely convinced that I was responsible and was dragging me off to the headmaster despite my denials when, in desperation, as I saw the inevitability of the cane which I had never experienced before, I landed a reflex punch on the end of her long and rather hooked nose. I do not think that a ten year old could have punched very hard but, as luck would have it, I had broken the bridge of the horn-rimmed glasses that she always wore and which contributed so much to her witch-like looks. For the next month or so until repairs could be effected she continued to wear these with a piece of sticking plaster to hold the two halves together.

If I had been innocent before, I was now for the high jump. I was sent into a room in solitary confinement awaiting the judgement of the Head, which seemed to take a very long time, and I am sure the waiting was worse than the execution. Mrs Lee was not very popular with the staff and I am sure, with hindsight, that the Head was trying to suppress his amusement as he interviewed me. He was very fair and heard me out, which was more than Mrs Lee had done, and I am convinced that he believed my side of the story; but hitting a member of staff could not go unpunished. I was given six strokes of the cane straight away which relieved the agony of any further waiting and I am convinced that he was lenient when I compare the after effects with other, more justified, canings that I later received. I became an instant hero to the other boys for the next two days and whatever the headmaster said to Mrs Lee must have had some lasting impact as, from then on, she no longer picked on me.

14. The Norfolk Broads

Dad chose to cruise the Norfolk Broads for the Easter holidays but, just like Dad, where everyone else would book a week, Dad booked three weeks on the tiniest and most ramshackle motorboat which had the very appropriate name of *Ragamuffin*. This fitted in with his need for peace and quiet with his family after the years of deprivation as a prisoner of the Japanese but also fitted in with his restless desire to explore and his love of nature, particularly birds. We explored every nook and cranny of the Broads and the river system that supported them. We went up the rivers Ant, Bure, Yare and Waveney and any smaller tributary until the shallow *Ragamuffin* grounded and had to be poled round for the return journey. In 1946 the Broads were uncontaminated with all the run-off from the farms which now produce a soup so rich in nutrients that the watercourses and lakes are an impenetrable sludge of algal growth. Then, one could see deep down into the crystal clear water with its abundant varieties of water plants, fish and other small aquatic creatures. We particularly liked to see the roach, with their blood red fins and shimmering silver bodies, as they swam in considerable numbers lit by the glancing sunbeams that penetrated the water.

Harvey and I decided that we wanted to fish for these and being miles from civilisation, we had to resort to an oar from the dinghy as an improvised rod, a bent pin and some thread from Mother's sewing box. We were anchored for the night on Barton

Broad, which was shallow and reed fringed, and had a light beige-coloured bottom from the rotting reed debris which showed up the fish nicely. We found that a pin without a barb was useless, in that the fish would take the bait and then slip off the hook. This required the application of lateral thinking and we developed the technique of watching for the instant the fish took the bait; and then we would yank the line hard, and by describing a large arc with the rod, to literally try to land the fish in the boat. We were only successful on two occasions and there must have been a number of puzzled fish who experienced the same sensations as tropical flying fish taking to the air. The technique required a great deal of concentration and could not be sustained for long.

Ragamuffin came cheaply; very necessary if one was hiring her for three weeks, and this showed. She was smaller than most of the other boats and was one of the oldest in service. Her accommodation was minimal, consisting aft of a small stern cockpit with a boxed in diesel engine, the wheel from which she was steered and boxed in benches along two sides and across the stern, which housed the gas bottles and other equipment. The main cabin had two bunks which my parents used and which doubled up as seats for the dining table placed between them and, just forward of this, there was a minute galley and sink on one side and a hand pumped toilet on the other. In the bows there was a very small cabin in which we slept, with an escape hatch and two bunks following the curve of the bow. The whole boat was lit by Calor gas lamps with mantles. The toilets at that time discharged straight into the water and it was not advisable to swim in the neighbourhood of boats. Not that one would want to in April in East Anglia.

Dad's insistence in going to the very limits of the river systems inevitably meant that we caught up large quantities of water weed round the propeller and the boat became slower and slower until Dad found that by slamming the engine from forward to reverse several times in quick succession, he could unwind the worst of the weed and restore some forward progress. But this process on such an old boat soon lead to a breakdown. The first one was not too serious as Father spotted that the pin securing the gear lever to the shaft of the gearbox had sheared. A simple phone call to the boatyard soon had a new one delivered and fitted and the fitter must have presumed that the cause was just old age. The second time, Dad's efforts to clear the weed with his unique method, suddenly had the engine accelerating to deafening revolutions with the boat remaining totally immobile. Something drastic must have happened and there was only one thing for it. Dad had to strip to his underpants and, tied by a rope round his waist for safety, he had to go over the side into the freezing water to investigate. He found the propeller covered in a football sized mass of weed and there was nothing for it but to take in large breaths and duck below the water and painstakingly remove the weed a handful at a time. When he had done this, he found that the propeller would spin freely on its stationary shaft. His unusual technique for freeing weed had successfully broken the shear pin that united the rotation of the propeller and shaft.

He emerged blue and shivering and was probably in the first stages of hypothermia. Mother wrapped him in blankets and plied him with hot cups of tea which, as a teetotaller, was probably better for him than neat whisky or brandy. Another phone call meant that we were towed to the nearest boatyard and the boat hauled out of the water for the repair to be completed. No underwater repairs for the local boatmen even though it was a five minute job to replace the pin. They had more sense!

Ragamuffin towed a dingy and we would take turns to ride in it, observing the water rushing by at near eyelevel and experimenting with hauling in the tow rope, while the bow wave surged almost over the stem. When we had hauled the dinghy to the point where it was almost touching the speeding *Ragamuffin*, we would abruptly release the rope, so that the dinghy hurtled back and came to a jarring stop as it reached the end of the slack in the towrope.

Father used to allow us to take turns in steering *Ragamuffin* and it was great fun to be in charge and sail under low bridges, like the one at Potter Heigham, with just enough clearance for the cabin. There, the sailing boats would have to lower their masts and sails and a skilled crew would do so underway and be carried under the bridge by their own momentum. Then, without a pause, they would re-erect the mast and sails while still moving and be on their way.

Some of the Broads had very narrow entrances through the reeds, and on one occasion we had passed such an opening around a bend on the way up the Waveney, and I had noted it. It was well up the river, where it was very narrow and twisty. On the way back I came to the bend that I thought I recognised and turned the boat hard round for the entrance to the Broad, where we intended staying overnight. The entrance was not there and we were heading straight for the sloping, muddy riverbank at full speed and there was not a thing that I could do: it was too late to throw the boat into reverse. There was a huge bang and the crash of things falling inside with the bows slicing and skidding through the mud, only stopping at an acute angle when two thirds of *Ragamuffin*'s hull was resting firmly on the bank; and all the while, curious Friesian cows looked on. It took Mum at the tiller with the boat full speed in reverse and her three menfolk pushing from the bank to release it; and then it nearly repeated the incident in reverse on the far bank, but Mum was somehow able to swing the boat round and stop it. Mum duly collected us from the bank in a more gentle manner and eventually found the correct entrance to the Broad. Dad did seem to be very tolerant of the broken crockery and jam jars; but then he had had his own misadventures!

15. Summer 1946

My recollections of that first summer at school in England was of endless watercolour blue-washed skies. Those were the days of double summer time and the evenings seemed to go on forever with it still being light long after we had gone to bed. That was the problem: it was so light and so hot in the dormitories that we could not sleep. Having finally put our lights out at nine o'clock, the staff would at last sit down to their evening meal; and it was well worth the long wait in austerity post-war Britain with its severe rationing.

Soon after they had sat down, we would creep down the corridors connecting the dormitories with the dining room and peer through the very small clear sections in the pattern of the frosted glass panes that made up the doors to the dining room. We would watch with great interest the progress of the staff meal as it went from soup to roast chicken with roast or new potatoes and fresh peas: chicken being a great delicacy at that stage of rationing. Or they might have some other roast joint with smells that would be unbearable, in contrast to our continual diet of boiled meats and vegetables. This would be followed by a sweet of fresh strawberries from the headmaster's garden, or they might have ice-cream or a fruit jelly and the meal would be concluded with coffee, probably ersatz Camp coffee made from chicory.

Sometimes we were caught peering through and then it was the headmaster's slipper for the delinquent and one would never know when one of the staff would mount a random check on what was going on in the dormitories. A number of us had torches with which we would read under the bedclothes but we would usually be caught if a staff member came in. I suppose the bedclothes stopped the light from scattering too far and gave some chance of an early warning if, on hearing the approach of a master, a KV (from Latin, *cave* = beware) was given by an alert boy stationed down the corridor. If he was to avoid detection himself, the sentry would need to be nimble and quiet as he ran back to his own bed in his bare feet. The slipper applied to a bare bottom by the headmaster was the usual punishment for not too serious misdemeanours and the number of whacks would depend on how horrific the crime was. The slipper was not too bad in that it stung with considerable pain but was only momentary and five minutes after the ordeal you could forget it. The cane was much more serious and was reserved for the most outrageous offences. Its effects were with you for a day or two and you had great difficulty in sitting for that period.

Our meals consisted of porridge and toast and margarine with a small dollop of jam for breakfast and, for a treat, a boiled egg thrown in on Sunday. Lunch consisted of stringy or fatty boiled meat, never roasted; or boiled fish accompanied by mashed or boiled potatoes, mashed swede or turnip, boiled cabbage and on rare occasions, carrots or peas followed by a proper pudding. Puddings were spotted dicks, a sultana suet; roly-polies; apple dumplings and other steam puddings of various sorts; sago, semolina or tapioca, known to us as frog's eggs; and detested rhubarb or prunes with custard. The suet based puddings were much appreciated in winter, providing the necessary calories for the cold. Quite often we would be given whale meat diced into centimetre sized cubes. It is hard to believe that this oily, dark-coloured, fatty meat with its distinctive strong flavour should be considered a delicacy by the Japanese. We hated it and, so, much of it went to waste. High tea consisted of sardines or corned beef, often in the form of fritters, or scrambled egg on toast followed by bread and jam or by bread and dripping to fill up on. The jam was invariably red, made from some root crop such as swede dyed appropriately, and had artificial seeds to simulate raspberry jam, and the dripping was mainly beef but sometimes came from other joints. Dripping was the congealed fat that had run off joints as they were roasted. The scrambled egg was made from dried eggs which came in a tin, the contents of which looked just like custard powder. Fresh eggs were so scarce that every recipe requiring eggs would have this substitution made and the taste was not a little strange. Certainly, in the case of the scrambled eggs, the fine powder would not reconstitute to the required consistency and often would have large lumps within it. We only ever had cake at the beginning of term, when mothers would bake their offspring a large solid cake in which dried eggs were a main ingredient, and this could be made to last a long time with careful eking out. All this food was brought up from the kitchens on a rope-operated dumb waiter, a small service lift which we all took turns to haul up by its counterbalanced endless-loop rope. After meals, we would have various duties, one of which was to load the lift with all the dirty crockery for washing up.

Though the food described may not have seemed too bad, if perhaps a little bland, because of rationing, the quantities of anything desirable such as meat, butter, eggs, coffee or sugar were minute. This was made up for by the relatively unlimited quantities of root crops, green vegetables and bread. To a nutritionist the diet was a very healthy one but to us it was insipid and monotonous.

The Canadian government had shown great generosity in sending to the schools of Britain, during those first post-war years, large tins of drinking chocolate, and this, together with our dessertspoon of malt, our teaspoon of cod-liver-oil and our vitamin C ration of Ministry of Food orange juice, was dispensed immediately after high tea. The chocolate had to be made to last as long as possible as we were each given two teaspoonfuls of the powder, placed in the palm of our hand. This was achieved by licking an index finger, dipping it into the powder and placing it into one's mouth; there to be savoured until the repeated operation finally exhausted the supply. Malt and orange juice, though strangely flavoured because of the added vitamins, were OK; but the cod-liver-oil was disgusting. Occasionally our pocket money, after several weeks saving, would run to a small tin of sweetened condensed milk and again the dipping finger would come into its own and we would see how long we could make a tin last.

Memories of a long hot summer are not made up of snatched glimpses of staff eating excruciatingly desirable meals, however. The memories come back to me as a succession of lazy days spent on the cricket field under blue skies watching the progress of the game which seemed to have no urgency to reach any conclusion. And when we got bored with our compulsory viewing of the game we would be entertained by the frequent aerial displays overhead. The war had ended less than a year before and the playing field was close to one of the aerodromes from which experimental aircraft were tested, possibly Elmdon, which at that time was not an airport but a small private airfield which had presumably been commandeered by the Air Ministry.

We would watch the early jet fighters, Meteors and Vampires, streak overhead with a deafening whine at low level leaving dirty smoke trails behind; or it might be the latest version of the Spitfire or the new contra rotating prop aircraft flying, by then, at a not much slower speed; with the characteristic tortured scream of the high revving piston engine operating at its limits. Occasionally we would be startled by the passage of the 'Flying Wing' in a sedate and high orbit over our heads. The 'Flying Wing' was literally that, with no fuselage and tail, and many, probably six, prop-driven engine nacelles spread over the length of its wings and, because of its experimental nature, it flew at a great height in case anything went wrong. We were often distracted by small private aircraft, invariably bi-planes and most often Tiger Moths, practising circuits and stunts at low level overhead, to the annoyance of the keener cricket fans but much appreciated by the rest of us. Presumably these stunts, which included loops, were not welcomed over their own airfield but our sports ground gave them an opportunity to practise in comparative security knowing that they had somewhere to land in an emergency.

The cricket pitch had a white painted wooden scoreboard attached to the shed in which the score keepers sat. I was no good at playing but I did enjoy filling in the scorebook and replacing on the scoreboard the black metal plates with their white numbers to register the latest score. Also on the pitch surround was, upended, a large metal roller with a long wooden box across its width which could be filled with more or less stone ballast, depending on whether a heavy or a light roll was required. An army of small boys would be recruited from time to time to man this roller and heave down on its shafts before beginning to roll the pitch accompanied by much shouting of commands and excitement. The remaining distraction from the match was the large pile of grass mowings into which we would dive and spring back and where, if one excavated deeply, the grass would be incredibly hot as it decomposed to compost.

For the serious, there were two practice nets but for those like me, these were to be avoided at all costs. Who in his right mind would place himself in the line of fire of a heavy ball being hurled at them with no possibility of escape; and being on the receiving end as a close fielder in front of a batsman was even worse. At least the batsman had pads and gloves. The poor fielder had none. I quite liked bowling because I thought it reasonably safe but the chances of getting a sustained spell at this were few and far between. The trouble with schoolboy cricket is that it is in the hands of a few cronies whose fathers can influence the sports master into thinking that their Johnny has a good record in the game. My father, living abroad, could not do this and the result was that I would be put in as ninth or so in the batting order and the side would be out before I had a chance to show my capabilities. I am saying this tongue in cheek because my brother Harvey, from the same handicap, eventually became good enough to be picked for the school team.

The highlight of the cricket season was the School versus Parents match. That first summer we had an American boy with the strange sounding name of Laimbeer, whose father worked as a diplomat of some sort in Birmingham. Despite the very English nature of the game, Laimbeer senior was picked for the parents' team. Up to this point the game had been a very ordinary but close fought one, but when Laimbeer senior came in to bat, he was armed not with a cricket bat but with a baseball bat. With his first ball, he ran right up the pitch and hit the ball cleanly for a six before it had time to bounce. To great cheers from the parents, he repeated this twice more, until the bowler for the school team got his brain into gear and delivered him a ball that ran along the ground, under his elevated bat, and the wicketkeeper was easily able to stump him while he was out of position halfway up the pitch. I do not remember who won the match.

Behind where the spectators sat, at the boundary of the cricket field, was the headmaster's fruit and vegetable garden and one of the distractions from watching the game was to sneak a strawberry from under the fruit netting behind our backs. Unfortunately, I was not very experienced at this and got caught redhanded but not before I had sampled the large ripe fruit. I was reported and this time, unlike the incident with Mrs Lee's spectacles, the head gave me a lecture on stealing and applied the cane with full force so that I was no longer a false hero but knew exactly how it felt.

Opams and Bundu Beetles

There was one form of cricket which we all enjoyed – paper cricket. This was a game of creating scores from the throw of dice and keeping a scorebook much like the real thing. We also kept minute statistical tabs of all our favourite teams, their individual batting and bowling averages and we were gripped by the postwar test matches with such famous names as Len Hutton, Sobers, Richie Benaud, Wally Hammond, Compton, Edrich, Graveney etc.

The final attraction of the playing fields were the bunkers formed by a number of long disused Anderson shelters on the extreme boundary between the end of the playing field and the next door paddock. I suspect that they were in the neighbour's ownership but we were not subject to such fine distinctions and so they were fair game. These bunkers were about six feet deep and we had cleaned them out in places so that they were once more connected and we then had a series of underground huts into which we brought torches and lit candles. I am sure the staff knew nothing of this, presuming that our activities would not extend onto someone else's property. We had our planned escape routes which would keep us ahead of any imaginary invaders and this was our den where we would pretend we lived, even bringing down bracken bedding and eating small snacks. This was the nearest I got to the freedoms of India and for many years I grieved over its loss. In India we could wander where we liked: here we could never leave the school except under escort and at prescribed times. It was a closed world and we were caged in.

It was in the middle of a class, in that summer of 1946, that I was called out of the room to be told of the death of my missionary grandfather in India. We had been very close to him during those years when Father was a prisoner of war and I just burst into floods of tears at the thought that I would never see him again. This was my first bereavement and I could now feel with another of the boys, Hawkins, whose father had died earlier that term from a heart attack while driving his car in a thunderstorm. Hawkins' father was in his early forties and he had to leave the school at the end of term because his mother could no longer afford the fees. My grandfather had at least died in relative old age from failing kidneys.

This was not to be the final heartache of that summer. We finished the Easter term with lessons from the young and healthy Miss Brown, our French teacher, only to come back to the summer term to hear that she was in an iron lung with polio. Poliomyelitis at that time was a killer and those who survived it often ended up as cripples unable to walk and, at best, to limp along in iron leg braces or on crutches. The iron lung was a great metal cylinder which was installed in some hospitals as a means for providing artificial respiration, as polio sometimes paralysed the chest muscles. It was not long into the term before we were given the sad news at school assembly that Miss Brown had died and prayers were said for her.

No term would end without the inevitable midnight feast by torchlight in the surrounding blackness of the night. Hoarded biscuits, sweets, an apple or pear etc. would be pooled and these would then be distributed, together with toothmugs of cordial, raspberry-ade or dandelion and burdock. The food was hardly gourmet but the thrill was in the daring, with the possibility of being caught *in flagrante delicto*, at an hour which to us was deliciously wicked.

The summer holidays were spent in Ireland, crossing over from Liverpool to Belfast, where we went on to the home of Father's youngest brother Albin and his Northern Ireland wife Grace, living there with their very young family. Grace started her life in the South. She was only a child at the time of the formation of the Irish Free State in the early 1920s, when her family, which was of Protestant origin, was displaced, and they were forced to make the move to the North. We only stayed with them for three days before we were again satisfying Father's wanderlust by exploring the Antrim coastline, the Giant's

Causeway and on through Londonderry to Lough Neigh. On the way up the Antrim coast, we had stayed at a guest house in Port Ballantrae, called the Red House, which catered for Christian families. My abiding memory of this stay was the solo by one of the lady guests during the evening get together in the lounge. She sang the hymn 'The Old Rugged Cross' with great verve and much feeling and sent us into fits of giggles as her large bosom heaved and wobbled as she delivered the piece in a deep, powerful tremolo. This style of fervent singing was fashionable at that time and large ladies who performed in this way were known to us as fruity contraltos.

The Red House was the base for rides on the rickety narrow gauge tramway that ran from Portrush to Bushmills, with its famous whisky distillery, and for visits to the Giant's Causeway, where the ranks of basalt hexagons, formed by the rapid cooling of molten volcanic rock, run gently down to dip below the surface of the Irish Sea and dramatically reappear on the Scottish island of Staffa, famous for Sibelius' setting of Fingal's Cave. It was also from here that we went on a vertigo-inducing crossing of a swaying rope bridge above a narrow channel, with the waves dashing below, to the small island of Dunluce with its castle mound and then we had to do it all again, to make the return passage back over the chasm.

From Londonderry we went on to explore Strangford Loch and its violently strong and dangerous rip tides as they debouched through the smallest of outlets to the sea; and then on through County Down until we finally ended up on a farm at the minute hamlet of Aughlisnafin, in a remote area of the county near Annsboro, with a backdrop of the Mourne Mountains close by.

Here there was an abundance of good farm food with the many Irish breads, including potato bread, buttermilk bread and soda bread, that are an essential part of an Irish tea. Here we were given honey, dripping from the comb, which had come

Summer 1946

*The re-united family one year after the end of the war.
(England, Summer 1946, just before Mother and Father's return to Malaya.)*

from the hives on the farm. We were to get to know that farm much better in later years and it seems impossible that the start of the days known as 'The Troubles' was some twenty three years into the future. Northern Ireland, then, was a beautiful and quiet place for a holiday.

We returned to school for the start of the winter term in the knowledge that Mother and Father had just three weeks left before they would have to leave for Malaya, for Father to recommence work which had been so precipitately interrupted by the war. They both had to collect and order everything that they would need for this new phase of their lives and complete all the formidable paperwork before the deadline. The day before they were due to sail, they came up to the Midlands *en route* for Glasgow, where they were to board ship, and spent one of those glorious early autumn days with us. The Head had given us permission to be away from school for the day and we made the most of it with walks and a meal out, and then it was time for our farewells. Mother was very upset. This was the second time that she had had to say goodbye to her young sons and this time it was for three years, which must have seemed to her like an eternity. We, on the other hand, had no idea what a three year gap would be like and we had been settled into the routine of term for some time. We were sad, but with no yardstick for comparison, we did not know what it would mean. Dad was loving but he did not reveal his feelings like Mother and, to this day, I do not know what that parting meant to him. They caught the bus outside the school gates where we waved them off and then we were absorbed into the tedium of evening prep. It was a wise move by the Head, as he knew that we would then not have time to dwell on our feelings.

16. Christmas

The end of term saw us being put on the train for Gosport for a journey that entailed a change at Warwick from the local stopping train to the express and, at London, a switch from the GWR Paddington terminus to the SR Waterloo terminus via the underground, followed by a disembarkation at Portsmouth Harbour station to walk down to the harbour ferry to cross to Gosport. The final stage was a local bus ride to Uncle Wilfred and Auntie Millie's new home at 25 Parham Road: an address that we had not yet seen. All this unaccompanied: myself aged ten with Harvey in tow. Nowadays it is hard to believe that a ten year old and a nine year old could do this in complete safety but we had tongues in our heads and everywhere we asked for directions we met with nothing but kindness and help. Complete strangers would make sure that we got onto the right connection and would often accompany us to see that we did so, even though it meant that they had walked well out of their way. Our luggage, consisting of large cabin trunks, had been sent on ahead by PLA – passenger luggage in advance – and so we had travelled light with only a small bag each.

The Parham Road house was a typical Edwardian semi of which there were thousands of identical copies throughout England. It had been the builder's own house and so had some desirable extras including a large conservatory with a mature vine that produced a crop of blue-black grapes in abundance. Despite being fully plumbed with an upstairs loo and bathroom, it also had a brick privy and coal shed at the bottom of the substantial garden together with a well built summer house which Harvey and I occupied as a bedroom in summers to come. This came equipped with a full sized wrought iron double bed, in which we slept, liberally supplied with decorative threaded, brass knobs. We would unscrew these and then screw them back on so as to help while away those light summer nights when we could not get to sleep for heat and the sustained caterwauling of the lovesick tom cats that proliferated in the area. But that was later. For this winter and succeeding winters we slept in the loft among the jumble that had collected over time. This arrangement had its advantages for it was here that our own cabin trunk of toys lived and, if we were restless at night, this and some of the other junk found there could be explored at leisure until we were ready to nod off.

The house had the usual narrow two storey frontage of that era forming the top of a T with rooms left and right of the entrance hall. Then, extending a long way back as the tail of the T, came the breakfast room, kitchen and laundry room cum pantry. The conservatory was built onto the side of these rooms with direct access from the breakfast room. It also meant that the house was better insulated on that side.

Upstairs there were bedrooms and a bathroom occupying the same floor plan and above the two front bedrooms was the loft in which we slept which had a very steep and narrow enclosed staircase with a door at the bottom. This was not a loft built for the maids and had never been intended for occupation. There was no insulation in the roof apex and it was lit by a single bulb and a skylight facing the rear of the house. Again, a double bed had been put here for us to sleep in, and it must have been cold, but I do not recall it so and, of course, Gosport had an equable climate on the south coast, being surrounded by sea.

As an Army Scripture Reader, Uncle used to host regular gatherings of men and women from all the services of this vast naval and military base area, which also included several air strips and Service hospitals. Not only did he and Auntie entertain them and provide the atmosphere of a home, which many had not experienced for a long time, but somehow they managed to supply them with sandwiches and cakes despite the stringent rationing of the time. I can remember some of the tricks used to make things go further. Cheese sandwiches, which I helped to make, where a minimal amount of cheese was diluted with a considerable amount of semolina and great spoonfuls of mustard to draw out what little flavour remained. These, together with Marmite sandwiches, sandwiches from home grown tomatoes with plenty of pepper added, bread and dripping, all accompanied by lashings of tea, were handed round. The food tasted good, especially after the fellowship of twenty or more young service men and women singing their hearts out to rousing choruses and Moody and Sankey's Victorian hymns of triumph from *Sacred Songs and Solos*. Uncle had perfect pitch and could play anything by ear even if he had only heard it once before. If the group was small and we were in the lounge, he would play his beloved piano but, when it was a large group, we would go into what was originally the dining room, now converted into a meeting room with utility chairs and a pedal organ which he used with great gusto.

After his encounter with Christianity during the First World War and the change this had made to his life, Uncle wanted to become a missionary. He had been a soldier in General Allenby's command and he was present in the march into Jerusalem after its siege had been raised. On completion of his initial training, he was sent out as a Plymouth Brethren missionary to the Godavari river delta in the early 1920s, the same mission field in which my grandfather served. They would have had frequent contact with each other but would not have known that some years later the one would become the father-in-law of the other. Sadly within a year his first wife, who had accompanied him together with their young family, became seriously ill and was told by the doctor that she could not continue living in the heat of India. She and her children had to return to England immediately and, by coincidence, they travelled on the same ship as my grandfather and his family who were returning on furlough. They got to know each other well. In that family was my father's sister Millie, a young girl who many years later Uncle was to marry. Uncle followed his wife home a year later and, soon after his arrival in England, he transferred to SASSRA, an acronym for the Soldiers and Sailors Scripture Readers Association, where his zeal to be a missioner would be put to the test: but his heart remained in India. His postings thereafter were to the various military garrison towns and ports of England with just the one spell in Gibraltar.

He was very good at his job which entailed going into all the service establishments: hospitals, barracks, naval and air bases etc. and conducting services, often at the invitation of the base chaplain; distributing scriptures and tracts; providing counselling and generally offering a home for the young conscripts to come back to in their off duty moments for warmth and company. This even extended to the German prisoners who served a period of reparation in Britain immediately after the war and who kept up the link for several years after in correspondence and visits.

In the mid 1930s his wife died from an undiagnosed perforated stomach ulcer and he married my aunt while he was stationed in Morecambe in 1941. She was the young girl who had travelled on the ship with his family ten or fifteen years earlier when they had returned to England. Some time after their marriage, he was moved down to Gosport where Harvey and I later came on the scene.

Our first Christmas at 25 Parham Road was to be an eye opener for us. Uncle was a Victorian, brought up in rural Devon, and Christmas was celebrated in the Dickensian fashion with all the trimmings, including the goose. It all began several days before with a huge effort at decorating every inch of the house with streamers, holly and mistletoe, and the Christmas tree with fairy lights, tinsel, streamers and baubles. The tree would be a real fir, as large as the lounge ceiling would allow and on to it would be tied all sorts of presents, neatly wrapped and labelled, with larger ones at its base. The celebrations would start on Christmas Eve with the family, joined by a gathering of servicemen and women, singing Christmas carols round the tree, supplied with a generous quantity of mulled home-made wine sprinkled with grated nutmeg, accompanied by scones and sandwiches. There would also be bowls dotted around the room with sultanas, boxes of dates, nuts, dried figs and grapes. He was nothing but generous. His technique for mulling was to heat the poker in the coals of the open hearth and plunge this into the tureen of wine. The evening warmed up and the singing got more and more enthusiastic, until a halt was called for a reading round the fire, in his soft Devonshire accent, of his favourite Jan Stewer stories, based upon the comic activities of his native country folk in the area of Widdicombe by Dartmoor. This was followed by a short reading of the Advent story and by a benediction and the reluctant departure of the guests; while we all trooped off to bed.

We children should have been very tired but we were so excited in our anticipation, with our empty stockings hanging at the end of our beds, that we took a long time to go to sleep. We chose the largest stocking we could find in the hope that it could contain more. Indeed, a year or so later, I can remember still being awake when Uncle and Auntie crept into the bedroom to fill the stockings; and my waiting in feigned sleep until they had gone out. I then used my torch to examine the contents of my bulging stocking. Clearly, we had passed the stage where we believed that Father Christmas came down the chimney and we knew the mechanics of how the stockings got filled.

Those stockings contained a selection which might include sweets, tangerines, chocolates, nuts, a yo-yo, some marbles, Chinese puzzles of twisted interlocked wire loops to be unravelled, or small presents of the Christmas cracker variety: a small plastic magnifying glass, a miniature toy car, a whistle etc. But better still, at the foot of the bed, were a few larger presents to keep us quietly happy at this very early hour, until such time as the grown-ups woke up. I had a Waterman fountain pen with a bottle of blue-black ink. Clever stuff this blue-black ink. When you wrote it was blue and about half a minute later it dried black. Keeping the nib below the surface, and squeezing the internal rubber tube by means of the lever on the pen barrel, would suck up ink to refill the pen in just the same way as squeezing the bulb on an eye dropper. One fill would probably last a week of normal use at school.

The other treasured present was a cheap wind-up Timex pocket watch with luminous dial and hands. It was enormous and glowed incredibly brightly in the dark. It was so radioactive that I am sure a Geiger counter would have registered right off the scale. I later bought a leather strap to hang it from my lapel where it nestled in the top pocket of my coat. The timekeeping would be accurate to within five minutes each week which was fine for a young lad.

Christmas morning breakfast was a light affair to be hurried through, as we were all anxious to open the main family presents before setting off for the morning service and the later chores of Christmas dinner. We assembled in the lounge and then we would hand round, in turn, our own presents to the recipient. These were opened in front of everyone so that all could share in each other's delight and perhaps be a little envious. For both of us from India, this was a completely new experience as we had not previously exchanged or received presents at Christmas. We were intrigued by the large square box that was labelled for us and which we found was from Mum and

Christmas

Dad, who had ordered it before they had left for Malaya. It was a simple oval layout of a three rail electric Hornby '00'-gauge model railway with a green LNER tank loco, three trucks and a guard's van. We also received from other members of the family two or three Dinky cars, a set of lead farm animals and a set of railway staff: porters, guards, stationmaster and the like. We never stopped playing with our railway and each subsequent Christmas bits were added to it until it became a sophisticated layout with points and sidings, two engines, coaches, a tunnel and so on, together with many Dinky toys, including aircraft of that time. I see these same model cars, trucks and planes nowadays, displayed in locked cabinets in antique shops, commanding considerable sums of money.

Our Christmas lunch was traditional and we all wore paper hats from the crackers we had just pulled. Though teetotal, apart from his occasional indulgence in home made wine, Uncle was not averse to flaming the brandy that he poured over the Christmas pudding. Within this pudding were hidden silver threepenny pieces which we were enjoined to look out for and which Uncle exchanged for the then current, frilly-edged, bronze ones. The originals would be set aside for the next Christmas. The lunch, followed by an enormous washing up session in which everyone helped, was completed by a mandatory armchair snooze for the adults before the King's speech and the later, but essential, walk to shake it all down.

It seems incredible that after all this indulgence there would be an evening tea around six, with homemade brawn, the highly spiced and jelly encased mixture of the gleanings of meat from the boiled head of a pig or sheep: not a favourite with us two. There would be sausage rolls and sandwiches and a Christmas cake all eaten in the breakfast room, lit by an Aladdin oil-lamp, sat in the centre of the table, which gave a warm glow to the proceedings. All our teas were eaten in this room by the light of the oil lamp and were accompanied during the week by the

'Children's Hour' radio programme and following on later, 'Dick Barton – Special Agent'. This tea was ended with a reading from the Bible followed by a short prayer from either Uncle or Auntie.

The long but happy day was finally concluded by yet more carols around the Christmas tree, mulled wine and mince pies and the giving out of those last few token presents from the tree. The carols reminded us of why we celebrated Christmas and Uncle would draw it all to a nostalgic conclusion with his own very appropriate epilogue. It was a weary drag to bed where we fell asleep the second our heads touched the pillow.

17. The Terrible Winter of 1947

Back in the form room, looking out of the window in a bored moment at the leaden grey sky, with the garden cedars so black that no detail could be seen beyond their silhouettes, I suddenly realised that minute white flakes, thinly dispersed, were drifting slowly across the black background of the trees. They were invisible against the grey of the sky. The next time I looked out, they had become bigger and it was not long before the flakes had become huge flocculant lumps of candy floss so big as to float down in a yawing motion and the air was filled with them. They just kept coming and coming and by now the whole class had become interested, including the teacher. Though we had not seen snow in India, I do not think that the other boys had seen snow quite like this in England. It settled incredibly quickly and before the day was out there was about two feet on the flat areas of the lawn and the drifts were as much as five feet deep. I thought this was normal English winter weather, as the only snow we had seen before was on Christmas cards and these usually showed Santa looking down the chimney of a thickly snow covered house, or a robin on holly bushes observing coaches stuck in huge drifts of the stuff.

Excitement mounted and our attention wandered from the lesson, as we could hardly wait for the next break when we could all stream out and sample the delights of this new phenomenon. It was a strange sensation, new to me, to collect large handfuls of loose snow and to feel it compress into a tightly bound lump of

Opams and Bundu Beetles

much denser mass, as I kneaded it into the desired shape, or rolled it along the ground to gather mass and form a huge snowball. The huge snowball would then become the body or the head of a snowman or would form the basis of a primitive igloo or some other product of the imagination. It would not be long before all this activity would degenerate into a melee, as snowball fights developed, with boys chasing each other up and down the playground in furious skids as each tried to escape the other in tight turns with no grip beneath their feet. The asphalt playground proved ideal for slides as the snow compressed to ice, where our momentum carried us forward after the initial run up, and we soon learnt to make these slides even faster and more lethal by throwing a bucket of water down their length.

Harvey and I quickly found that we could not take very much of this as our veins, used to the watery blood of India, were inadequate to provide the necessary circulation to our hands and feet to keep them warm. The agony that developed in our extremities was excruciating and re-entering the warmth of the buildings only made it worse. It must have been akin to the mediaeval torture chambers where a vice was slowly and inexorably tightened on finger ends and toes and, when the worst of the pain was over, the sensation was one of hands and feet glowing pink and burning hot. Wet gloves had not helped and most of the English boys discarded such impediments because their circulations, accompanied by such violent exertions, were able to cope with the conditions. We soon discovered chilblains on fingers and toes, which became extremely tender and would itch unbearably as they warmed up.

Our expeditions to the village were now through canyons of snow on the footpath, where workmen had shovelled a narrow path through and piled the surplus either side. Snowploughs had cleared the centre of the road just enough for one vehicle to proceed, leaving the occasional wider passing section, and this had piled the snow along the road edges higher than we could see over. There was no de-icing salt available and walking on these icy pavements became an art which had to be mastered if you were not to fall over or progress too slowly. The roadway itself would be covered in a thin film of compressed snow that the snowploughs had left. Fortunately there were very few cars on the roads so soon after the war and the extreme conditions meant that only those with an essential mission would be out. These few had their tyres encased in chains for grip and we would hear them jingling towards us from a long way away. It was this scarcity of vehicles that drew our attention to the solitary taxicab weaving its way down the cleared track. It had a platform built on its roof, holding up a large canvas bag ballooning half-full with gas. The gas was town gas from the coke plants and was being used as an alternative fuel at this time of petrol shortage.

Heating became a problem for most people that winter as coal stocks ran out and what there was was diverted to the power stations. The school had enormous stockpiles of coke for the boilers well before the winter began, but even this had to be eked out, as there was no possibility of replacing the stock once it had been used. The radiators never felt very warm but this may have been a product of the many power cuts which were initiated to ration electricity by a rota system. The power stations had insufficient coal to keep running continuously and each area had to take its turn in being shut down for some hours. Whether our central heating system relied on electric circulation pumps, or was based on convection, might have determined why the heating system was running at such a low ebb. Luckily the dormitories for the youngest boys were in the most modern extension of the school and had reasonable insulation. The older boys, as a privilege for their seniority, were housed in much smaller groups of three or four in the attic bedrooms of the old house where the former servants lived. These rooms in the roof space had no insulation and were freezing.

That winter seemed to go on and on and my recollection was that it only ended just before the Easter holidays and I have visions of roads and footpaths like running streams as the hot early April sun began the rapid thaw.

England had revealed another of her surprises in the vastly contrasting seasons, each of which had its own contribution to the wonder and pleasures that come with change. Even November, with its short, cold, dank, fog-bound days, could bring real comfort as one had the excuse to do nothing more than sit reading a book in front of a blazing coal or log fire.

18. The Staff

The staff were a very mixed group. There was Colonel Sadgrove, a hardened ex-Indian Army Officer, middle aged, very erect with a regulation army moustache, dark hair brushed severely to one side and kept in place with brilliantine and whose whole complexion was a deep mahogany with the wrinkled skin of a walnut. He taught us History, was very correct and exerted control effortlessly, as we were all a little overawed by him. Then there was Mr Gittings, in his early thirties, who had come from a school in Bournemouth with a reputation for strict discipline. His manner of drawing the wandering attention of a daydreaming boy was to hurl the wood and felt blackboard rubber, a solid object at least nine inches long by three wide, with great force and accuracy to just miss the miscreant and rebound off the folding wooden partition which divided our classroom from the next. The partition would act like a sounding box and magnify the booming sound of the impact to startle the lad into instant attention. The remainder of the class would have plenty of warning, as Gittings' voice would fade away as he focused his attention on his oblivious victim, picked up the board rubber, wound his arm back and executed a professional cricketer's throw. If the board rubber was not to hand then the chalk would do. What the master of the class in the room the other side of the partition thought of all this, which must have been totally disruptive to his class, I do not know, but Gittings continued to do this throughout his time at the school.

Mr Elliot was the French and Latin master and also ran the Cub Group, assisted by Miss Glazebrook. Another thirty year old, he was one of those very rugged dark-shadowed men who must have had to shave twice a day, and though just beginning to thin on top, would have made an excellent candidate as a film star. He had the looks that one associates with the Norman barons that came over with William the Conqueror and he must have spoken French much like one of them, with a very strong and slightly exaggerated accent. Miss Brown, who died so tragically, had been his junior French assistant. Mr Elliot was a man with a social conscience and was not given to using physical persuasion or correction. His preference was the issuing of lines or giving out detentions. The writing out of 500 lines could be a tedious affair and so we used our inventive minds to counter the problem. We cobbled together a lashing of four pencils on a cross-member, with the pencil points in alignment, so that we could write out, four lines at a time, the phrase that we had been given. Lines might well be, 'I must not chew toffees during the French lesson,' and this cunning device would reduce the effective punishment to only 125 repetitions of the phrase.

The bombardier, an ex-RAF Physical Training Instructor, otherwise known as Mr Wells, was the sports master responsible for all our games and the gym. He also doubled as carpentry master. He was a stocky man, proud of his sixteen stones of solid muscle and he was careful to let slip this fact on occasion so that we were all aware of it. He and Mr Coleman were the only married masters, living off the premises and in their own homes. The rest of the male staff were all bachelors and were to a lesser or greater degree eccentrics who had never fully grown up, except of course Mr Elliot, who was much sought after by the ladies and who eventually got married in my final year at Eversfield. Mr Wells was a typical NCO, blunt and to the point, who treated us young gentlemen as equals and stood no nonsense. My only clash with him was when I was in goal in

The Staff

one of our football matches and there had been very little activity at my end of the pitch. One of our backs, who had got thoroughly bored, started to act the part of a shunting engine and several times backed into me, moving his arms as though they were the pistons and cranks on a locomotive, accompanied by the appropriate choo-choo noises, and I had to fend him off each time he bumped into me. Wells, who was refereeing the game, heard the noise and on turning round, caught us both at the moment of collision. We were sent off the field but I refused to go, protesting my innocence. He ran over and picked me up like a feather, walked off the playing field and dumped me. It was no use protesting any further. Wells used to consider it manly for each of us to go into the boxing ring for three rounds. I hated boxing because I had a long nose that always formed a target for my opponent and which bled profusely every time it was hit. I was so scared into protecting this nose that I was incapable of mounting an attack which might at least have prevented further damage and I eventually had to have it cauterised twice. I was good at gymnastics, being light and agile, and so restored my place in his favour. He was an expert at catching us in vaults from the box or other apparatus, which made us fearless and prepared to try anything and, with his undoubted strength, he could pluck us out of the air no matter how fast we flew.

My other encounter with him was in the carpentry workshop where I was making a wooden tuckbox with rebated joints which required some fine chisel work for completion. Being right handed, I made the mistake of working across my body with the chisel, while holding the workpiece with my left hand, with the inevitable result that when the chisel slipped, it slashed across my wrist and cut right through the artery. It did not hurt immediately but blood was pumping out everywhere. Mr Wells flew across the workshop and had me in a tourniquet made from his handkerchief before I had even registered the true extent of the damage and I was whisked off in the headmaster's car to the surgery. Miraculously, none of the tendons or vital nerves had been damaged and I was sewn up with the next four stitches of my accident prone life.

Apart from Mrs Lee, the lady staff members all seemed quite normal and only Mrs Cardwell, the Matron, stood out in any way. Mrs Cardwell was a diminutive Welsh widow with white hair and a very pale complexion as though she never saw sunlight. She seemed far too old to have a son at school only a year older than me and one would not expect such a small frail, apparently elderly, lady to be able to control such energetic and mischievous youngsters. On the contrary, the sharpness of her tongue would command immediate obedience and even some of the more junior staff were in awe of her. She ran the sick bay and there was no malingering there. My encounters with the sick bay were a small selection of the usual sore throats, flu epidemics and quarantine illnesses that youngsters got before the days of preventative injections – measles, chicken pox, mumps etc. – and such was the influence of Mrs Cardwell, that I was relieved to get out as soon as possible. It was not that she was unkind, but that sick bed routines and the medicines of those days were not pleasant, injection needles were long, fat and very painful, your friends were not able to visit and you were not allowed out of bed. Boredom soon settled in and the only compensation was being allowed to read books.

19. Odds and Ends

The summer term saw the beginning of our swimming classes. We would assemble at the end of the track that ran into the playing field from Manor Road where an ancient pre-war coach was waiting. We would all pile into this while a roll call was taken before the coach set off up the Warwick road on its journey to Sparkhill baths. It seems strange that, fifty years later, two of my grandchildren should learn to swim in these very same baths. The journey seemed to take ages as we wound our way through prosperous suburbia, with relatively modern detached and semi-detached houses; through former village centres, now showing on modern maps as a line of shops swallowed up by the city; and on to older Edwardian and Victorian houses; and then through rows of terraces, slowly becoming more seedy, until we came to the baths set on the edge of a city park. There was a great rush to disgorge, to the shouted admonitions of the master in charge, who would be trying to exert control, and then we would be led to the changing rooms in mounting excitement. The baths had been booked for a closed session for the school and we were all frantically changing in the white tiled surroundings which acted as an echo chamber. Speed was essential if we were not to miss a second of the time allocated to us. The high pitched shouts and squeals would reverberate with increasing intensity over the water as we stepped into the pool area so that one could not hear anything that was said and it was only the frantic blast of the master's whistle that brought everything to a deafening silence.

Those that claimed that they could swim were singled out to do a demonstration width in the pool centre, while the beginners were sent to the shallow end for instruction. My half submerged swim in the lakes in India, just before the journey back to England, justified my claim to be a swimmer and I was sent off on my proving width, flailing my arms in a frantic effort to keep afloat and managing somehow to make it. I was pronounced a swimmer and left to my own devices with the other swimmers who could now enjoy relatively unsupervised fun. This consisted more in ducking and splashing each other than in swimming while staff attention was focused on the beginners. A very satisfactory state of affairs for us swimmers. Needless to say, changing at the end of the session was a much slower procedure, with many threats from the masters that anyone delaying the return of the coach would not be allowed to come next time.

Wednesday was a half day, when there would be no afternoon school, and the time would be spent in either a walk or a cycle ride on those occasions when there was not a school football or cricket match to support. For one of our regular Wednesday walks, we would set off down the playing field track and Manor Road and then head up a country lane, across the hump-back bridge over the canal, where there was a dock with a coke processing plant which had the unpleasant smell of rotten eggs. Canal barges would discharge their cargoes of coal for processing and the by-products were the large piles of coke from which the school would get its heating supplies. The gasometer was an interesting feature of the plant as it rose and fell according to the demand for town gas. These gasometers were layered cylinders, fitting snugly into each other like Russian dolls, with the last one having a cap so that the gas was contained in it. As more gas was produced, the whole lot would rise, each layer following the

Odds and Ends

previous one and, when the demand exceeded the supply, they would successively collapse into each other.

Beyond the canal we would walk along the lane to a wood which was one of our favourite play areas and would be allowed to run wild within it. Unfortunately this came to a sad end, when one of the boys came upon a couple within a coppice whom he thought were having a fight, with the man pinioning down the woman. He ran back to the master to have it stopped; but on returning to the scene the master interpreted the activity very differently! We later learnt from one of the senior boys what had really been going on.

On other occasions our half days would see us heading into the village to spend our pocket money. Our favourite destination was Woolworths, which then proudly proclaimed that it was a 'Threepenny and Sixpenny Store'. Every item in the shop was priced at either threepence or sixpence. This was a bit of a cheat because some items were split into a series of individual packets which all had to be bought to make up the whole, but generally the statement was true for those things that we were interested in. Our pocket money was very limited so there was not much room for extravagance.

There were numerous items that we coveted but the favourites were practical items with which we could make things: bulbs, switches, batteries, wiring bought off reels by length, brightly coloured hollow plastic tubing also on reels, sandpaper, screwdrivers, magnets etc. The electrical items were used to make various lighting systems that we could use in our dens or under our pillows when we wanted to read after lights out. The beauty of this approach was that we could gradually build up the lighting unit with our sixpences, whereas we would never be able to afford a torch outright. The plastic tubing was used for siphoning water from one level to another in what appeared to be an impossible condition where water seemed to go uphill. Perhaps the most clever of all the uses of this tubing, was to make a diver in a bottle. The diver was the globe of a burnt out torch bulb, with the end carefully broken off, so that water could enter into it. This was placed in a bottle of water where the amount of air trapped in the torch bulb was just enough for it to float. The first bottle was connected by a plastic tube, which ran as a tight fit through its cork top, to an open container of water above. This container could be raised or lowered, so that the water pressure in the sealed bottle below would increase or decrease. If it increased, the residual air in the diver (*bulb*) would be compressed and diminish in volume and so the diver would sink, or vice versa and it would float. The control of this system was tremendous, and one could have the diver hovering. The same effect could be obtained by just pushing a cork in and out of a bottle, but the control would be gone, and the diver would either sink rapidly, or get the bends as he hurtled to the top! We took great pride in injecting red, green or blue coloured inks into the water to enhance the effect.

Among the other items furnished by the threepenny and sixpenny store were Jews' harps which, when held between the teeth and plucked, emitted a twanging noise. Sometimes this discordant noise would continue into the start of a lesson which left a problem of detection for the master. There were tin frogs with a dimpled metal plate underneath, which made a loud click when pressed and, when combined with several others, could make an excruciating cacophony; magnetic ladybirds to stick to any convenient metal object; there were horseshoe magnets; toy cars, usually more primitive than Dinkys; small tin musical instruments that had a vibrating membrane, claimed by us to be made from the skin of a frog, which gave out a continuous drone that could be varied by finger holes: a sort of high pitched didgeree-doo; pens and pencils; kaleidoscopes; and even a thing with the impossible name of a 'Seebackroscope', which was a crude form of periscope that enabled you to see what was going on behind you.

Odds and Ends

One of the boys of scientific inclination had been given a chemistry set for his birthday. We all hung round to share in the various experiments from the selection of bottles containing crystals or powders of the various inorganic metallic salts, which when made up into solutions and mixed, would produce precipitates of the most colourful kinds. The blues and greens of copper, the red of chromium, black precipitates, white ones, the yellow of condensing sulphur smoke and the mystery of the pink of phenolthaline which, when acid or base was added in titration, would instantly lose all its colour or vice-versa, or that of litmus paper which turned red or blue in the presence of acid or base. The set contained glass test tubes and a methylated spirit burner and we were very envious of our friend Parker. In a neat row, nestled in hollows in the top of the cardboard base, were half a dozen stink bombs made of the most fragile glass which, when trodden on, were designed to shatter and release their contents of hydrogen sulphide to suffocate the classroom with the deadly smell of rotten eggs. It was this chemistry set that led to my later love of science and particularly chemistry.

Origami was put to good use as we made our paper aeroplanes, darts, sailing boats, animated flying birds, snappers that made a dull, but loud, clucking noise and not least, paper water bombs which were hurled around the classroom when the teacher was not present. Mother's early lessons in this art were not wasted.

Sometimes we would be walked to the Dove House Lane shops where there was no Woolworths and we would spend our pocket money on ice cream cornets, threepence for one scoop or sixpence for two. Dairy products were in short supply and the ice creams were very artificial in taste. We likened them to the imagined taste of Brilcreme, the popular men's hair pomade of that era.

On rare occasions we would catch the Midland Red bus into the Bull Ring in central Birmingham; and walk through the market areas behind St Martin's Church; and past the fishmongers' stalls which would be exuding into the gutters sluggish streams of grey sludge that smelt abominable. We would hurry past these to our destination, which might be John Lewis' Emporium or the shops in New Street. The Bull Ring was also the terminus for the many trams, with cables overhead, the connecting arms of which would have to be turned round by the conductor for the return journey. We were envious of their greatly superior acceleration over our buses and were very conscious of the smell of the electric sparks that they gave out in profusion. A tram ride was rare, but was something we enjoyed much more than a bus journey, and we were much more easily able to observe the driver operating the simple controls which we felt we could take over if the need arose. We did not come across trolley buses in Birmingham, but, in any case, these seemed tame and did not give off that excruciating squeal of the trams, as their tortured metal wheels took the tighter curves.

Coach trips were many, including one to Sutton Park, a remnant of Henry VIII's hunting forest which had originally stretched through Cannock Chase and occupied half of Staffordshire. The Park section was given to the Royal Borough of Sutton Coldfield by Edward VI through the influence of Bishop Vesey who founded the Grammar School there. Sadly, in Victorian times, there were many appropriations from the Park by the newly rich industrial magnates who wanted to build their homes overlooking this completely undisturbed forest land and only a very diminished portion remains. Nevertheless the remnant is about four miles in diameter and must look just as it did in Roman times, when the Roman road that still runs through it was a major highway. Traces of that highway are still very evident. Our visit would have been as a Cub Pack in uniform to carry out simple tasks of woodcraft and tracking. Other coach trips were taken to visit similar schools in the West Midlands as vociferous supporters of our own cricket or football teams.

Odds and Ends

On two occasions we went on a day's outing to Dudley Zoo. This entailed a change of train at Snow Hill. The line from Snow Hill ran for miles through the heart of the Black Country where, in the early nineteenth century, country folk for miles around, some as far as the Welsh borders and further, had flocked into the area which was fast becoming England's manufacturing heartland. They had come from the depressed rural communities seeking work in this rapidly expanding and brand new hive of industry, which was to provide so much of the wealth that later made Britain the foremost industrial nation in the world; and perhaps the first superpower. We passed factories belching out smoke of all colours in rising columns from tall brick chimney stacks. The commonest would be black or grey but occasionally there would be a sulphurous yellow or even the rare red or orange cloud of evil smelling vapour. The railway paralleled the canal, which had pioneered the route before the industrial revolution, in order to find a way through this industrial maze. We saw a steady stream of heavily laden barges making a slow but remorseless progress along the canal to the next factory basin, where they would moor and be unloaded. The surroundings of the factories were incredibly dirty with accumulated dust and this dust built up to cling to their outside walls. These walls were generally made from a skin of corrugated iron or asbestos on a framework of steel girders. In contrast, the interior floors of the factory were usually swept clean of detritus. We could look from the train windows straight into the core of the factories where the hangar like doors were invariably kept open, even in winter, to dissipate the tremendous heat from the furnaces. Great ladles would be pouring molten steel into moulds or we would see red glowing billets of the metal being passed through rollers to issue as rods or rails or some other product. When we made the return journey in the early dark of a winter's evening, the columns of smoke would glow with the reflected light from the furnaces, bright lit at their base gradually diminishing in intensity to where the column disappeared as a silhouette against the inky black sky. A modern Dante's Inferno, the whole effect heightened by the many reflections from the canals.

Dudley Zoo was set on the crest of a steep hill in the grounds of Dudley Castle which, from its great height, dominated the surrounding area. It was exciting running up and down the hill left to our own devices and looking at all the animals as we progressed around the site. The Zoo was very advanced for its time with its buildings and structures designed in the thirties by the avant-garde Russian born architect, Berthold Lubetkin. He was given the brief of creating 'a zoo without bars'. The animal enclosures were built into the hillside with high retaining walls and elevated observation platforms from which one had an excellent view looking down into them, and the enclosures attempted to emulate the natural environment from which the animals originated. Unfortunately, the celebrity of the architecture has meant that the structures are legally protected as an architectural and historic treasure and this has put a constraint on modernisation of the zoo. Any outing, particularly to a zoo, was fun but we could never make up our minds which was the true highlight of the day: the zoo or the train journey.

By this summer Harvey and I had made many schoolfriends and some, whose parents knew that our parents were abroad, were very generous in inviting us to their homes for tea or to birthday parties. Abrahams was a Jewish friend whose parents were extremely hospitable and they would invite a large number of boys round to their bungalow on his birthday. They were not obviously well off but they did not stint and, in those rationed days, they made the most of things that they could obtain off ration. Cucumber and tomato sandwiches figured large and they were delicious. Mrs Abrahams knew just what peppers and spices could make the most of what was basically very simple fare and her cakes were exceptional.

Schoolfriends at Eversfield. Back row (left to right): Akehurst, Lucani, Abrahams, Bromley III (Blake), Abraham's older brother. Front row: Bromley I, Teddy Jones, Bromley IV (Harvey). First names unknown!

Denby on the other hand came from a wealthy home. His father was someone big in industry and his parents ran a large Jaguar saloon car. Their home was one of the larger detached houses built between the wars, with many bedrooms and with generously sized ground-floor rooms. It had an extensive garden with a curved drive set in the most desirable part of the town. Mrs Denby loved entertaining and welcomed large numbers of boys at least once a term on one of our Saturday half days. Her meals were sumptuous, invariably with a starter course and twice I recall having asparagus tips dipped in melted butter followed by a huge roast and the sort of ice cream and jelly dishes that were favourites with us. We always left the table distended and only fit for the lightest of entertainment, which would sometimes come in the form of a conjuror, or the jerky images of a Korky the Cat or Walt Disney film in black and white, shown on their own home projector. Mrs Denby was plump and jolly as befits so generous a hostess, her husband was large and her son was a clone of these two amply proportioned people. Denby was a popular boy and his parties were very sought after.

The undisputed ring-leader of our set was Lucani, a half Italian boy with dark curly hair who was very precocious. He was stocky, with a strong physique, and had a round face and permanently healthy rosy cheeks and he had a boneless rubber ball of a nose which glowed with health. He was top dog of our little group and had the mischievous self confidence of someone who knew that he would not be challenged and he would quite often lead us into questionable, if not naughty, adventures.

Though we were a small, united band of friends, it now seems strange that we all addressed each other by our surnames. I had the unusual handle of Bromley III despite being the oldest of the four Bromleys at the school. The other two brothers, quite unrelated, had been at the school well before we arrived and so claimed the suffixes I and II. Can you imagine the affected tones of 'I say, Bromley III...' as one of my friends would address me. I used to cringe at the thought of these opening conversational words when years later I joined the Navy as an Ordinary Seaman for my National Service and mixed with my fellow countrymen from all walks of life. This proved to be a great leveller and I learnt to have a true regard for those I worked with from whatever level of society they came and it has significantly influenced my social attitudes and political leanings ever since.

During this summer, the dentist visited the school and possibly because there were four of us with the same name, I somehow got left off his list, with the result that during the nearly four years that I was at Eversfield I never once saw him. Harvey, who did see him, was given a brace to wear, consisting of a split palate which could be expanded with two adjustable nuts and it had a strong stainless steel wire which went across his teeth. Each week he would go through the routine of expanding the palate minutely until at the end of about a year, he had made sufficient room in his mouth to accommodate his previously crowded teeth. My earlier experience of the dentist in India led me to keep quiet and this had the disastrous effect of compounding a set of very bad teeth, which led later to numerous large fillings, with that of a very overcrowded mouth and severely impacted wisdom teeth. Years later these had to be removed under general anaesthetic and resulted in a damaged nerve so that a third of my tongue has no sensation of either taste or pain. I still have an overcrowded mouth and frequently bite my tongue, which swells and then gets sore and ulcerated because it has become too big for the space between my teeth. The temporary reprieve I gained from the dentist was not worth it.

The whole school attended singing classes which took place in the two form rooms in the new extension where assembly was held and where all school functions including concerts, prize-givings and dreaded examinations took place. The hinged wooden leaf partition separating the two rooms would be drawn back to provide the necessary space and a raised dais at one end provided the stage for performances.

With standing room only, books would be issued to a great hubbub of chatter and restless shuffling and then our music master would draw us all to a hushed silence while he announced the first song that we would practise. There would be a flourish of arpeggios from the piano followed by the louder introductory chord and we would all begin a spirited opening of:

> 'There came a knight all dressed in yellow,
> Fair are the flowers in the valley...'

Then followed several verses of knights of varying colours all performing various deeds of valour as they vied for the hand of the fair maiden. Suddenly there would be a great shout of 'Stop! Stop! You cannot sing it like that, the poor chap would never get his lady if you insist on dragging it so. Put some feeling into it'; and with that he would raise the tempo and we would all begin again. We sang all the old favourites. 'The British Grenadiers', 'O my Darling Clementine', 'The Minstrel Boy to the Wars has Gone', the stately opening to John Masefield's 'Cargoes':

> Quinquireme of Ninevah from distant Ophir
> ...with a cargo of ivory and apes and peacocks...

suddenly, in the last verse, bursting into the breathless staccato rush of:

> 'Dirty British coaster with a salt-caked smoke stack
> butting through the Channel in the mad March days.'

There would be 'John Brown's body lies a mouldering in the grave', the 'Londonderry Air', 'Loch Lomond' and fifty other tunes that every schoolboy of that era sang and which no one now knows. We enjoyed our singing as a break from the more serious pursuits of Latin and all its declensions or history with the sterility of all its dates, as it was then taught.

If music had ended with singing I would have been content but Father had paid for me to have piano lessons. With my retentive memory, I was great on theory but, when it came to playing, I was hopeless. I had inherited my mother's tiny hands with short fingers and found it very difficult to span an octave and chords of more than three fingers were impossible. My sense of rhythm and timing was non existent. The final humiliation came when we were supposed to play a piece in front of an audience of parents and the piece which I had practised so assiduously, knew by heart and could have played in my sleep, just dried up on me. After two abortive restarts I had to leave the room burning with shame and embarrassment.

The music room was on the third floor, next door to my favourite room in the long roof ridge space, which had recently been converted into the school library. I would spend most of my free time in the library delving in the rows of books on the shelves for yet another treasure. I read all the Captain Marryat sea stories and his *Children of the New Forest*; a few of Dickens' novels, which, for someone that young, was unusual; Arthur Ransome's stories of children's sailing adventures, set in the Norfolk Broads amid all the aquatic bird life of that area and, above all, every Biggles or Worrals book by Captain W.E. Johns that I could lay my hands on. In addition to the books there were the comics, the *Dandy*, the *Beano*, the longer stories of the *Champion* with Wilson the runner, and the *Boys' Own* with Billy Bunter and many others.

20. Summer Holidays

Two months of holiday is a long time to keep two energetic young boys occupied and so the period was divided up. Initially we returned to Gosport and set about rediscovering the joys of our unused toys. There was our Meccano set, a construction set of pierced metal strips, rods, angles, nuts, bolts and clips which could be made up into working models: much like modern Lego but which took far longer to assemble, as each nut and bolt had to be laboriously tightened with spanner and screwdriver. There would be the train set and stamp album and many other forgotten toys but after each of these had been played with once or twice, we would find the pull of the warm summer days too much to resist and we would look further afield.

Gosport and Portsmouth harbour were wonderful places to explore as there were constant ship movements to be watched and our road ran right down to the end of a muddy creek, one arm of many radiating out from the main harbour. In the creek were the ribs of old sailing vessels sticking starkly out of the mud with perhaps a remnant of decking. We would throw in baulks of timber from the flotsam at the water's edge, until we had made a causeway of stepping stones to the wreck, and then we would board with caution, as some of these hulks were not a little rotten. There would be the odd steel hull of a long since abandoned ferry boat which once plied across the harbour with its plates all sprung where rivets had popped. From the end of this creek we could see the four battleships of the British fleet which had been towed as far up the harbour as their draughts would allow and had then been mothballed. All their guns and radar turrets had been cocooned in a sort of plastic sheath which gave these protuberances the look of pupating insects stuck onto the enormous hulls. In addition to these there were a few old-fashioned yachts berthed in the creek and, when the tide came in, we would watch men row out to them and carry out various maintenance tasks, or occasionally raise the anchor and set sail across the harbour.

If we ventured further afield, it would be on the bus which ran through the High Street to its terminus at the harbour ferry just beyond. The High Street and its shops were of no interest to us as our sights were set on the jetty with all its activity. Perhaps the one exception was the camera shop. I had coveted the many cameras on display to satisfy my passion for photography, but the cost of them made this goal unattainable. I was only eleven, but two and a half years later my dream was fulfilled when Father, now back on leave from Malaya and knowing my interest, gave me a Coronet Cameo miniature camera for Christmas. This little camera, about two inches long, took still photographs using 8mm cine film and these miniature negatives had to be enlarged to make the then fashionable $3^{1}/_{4}$" x $2^{1}/_{4}$" prints. This extreme enlargement gave very fuzzy and flat results which made the pictures virtually indecipherable. Despite that I was very proud of that camera.

Walking back from the harbour, through the High Street and about half a mile beyond, we came upon the town park with a large oval pool, a favourite of retired naval officers, on which they sailed their sizeable home-made racing replicas, modelled on the Americas Cup and other racing yachts of the time, each with complete sets of sails. We were fascinated by these and in particular their self steering gear, which had many ingenious modifications to enable the boats to sail in a straight line down the course. The competitions were deadly serious and we had to be careful that we were not perceived to be a nuisance to these men of the sea, in their nautical caps, puffing their filled pipes of assorted aromatic tobaccos.

At the back of Uncle's house stood the tall flagstaff of HMS *Vernon*, the boy seamen's training establishment, behind its twelve foot high perimeter wall. We were sleeping in the summer house at the end of the garden just below this and would be woken up by the clear piercing call of reveille as the boys began their day. Throughout the rest of the day we would hear the bugle calls, each with its own message. 'Come to the cookhouse door, boys', or the call to muster on parade, or that final one at the end of the day, the haunting tones of the Last Post, with its notes fading and dying in tune with the fading light of the evening. Sometimes we would be able to see the boys manning the yardarms of this tall mast, frighteningly high above our heads, and then watch them limber down the ratlines in a continuous stream to the safety of the ground.

It was on our rare shopping expeditions to Portsmouth, to pick up replacements for outgrown items of school uniform, that we came across trolley buses and it was from the upper decks of these that we had our first glimpses of slums, the substandard housing for the poorest groups in society which were a legacy from the Victorian era. Often they were squares of terraced houses opening into enclosed courtyards, with only one exit and one privy for the whole block, and sometimes with only one external tap. It was not unusual for an extended family to be living in just two rooms. Very often it was the slums that took the brunt of the bombing, and this led to the more enlightened councils pulling them down wholesale and replacing them with new housing, in those early years after the war. Prefabs were an interesting example of these efforts. We had looked round one of these miniature homes that came as a factory, pre-built, sectional kit to be assembled on site. Very often they would be completed within one day after the construction of the base and the provision of services.

I keep painting Uncle as a paragon of virtues and have seldom mentioned Auntie. Perhaps this was because she would have had a hard task to stand out against his obviously extrovert and ebullient personality, but she was the quiet and cheerful administrative brains behind the partnership and, without the one half, the other would not have been nearly so effective. It was she whom we turned to as our second mother and it was she who saw to all our needs and arrangements both at home and in liaison with the school. Even now when she is in her late eighties and I am sixty three, I think of her as mother. Until three years ago, when she was eighty five, she was still the events organiser for the Sunrise Group of senior citizens of her village of Uffculme in Devon. She has a needle sharp brain and still loves any sort of intellectual quiz or conundrum.

Uncle's list of virtues is not yet complete. He was green fingered and devoted a great deal of time to the garden and his allotment. His gardening was completely organic using compost from trimmings and household waste, with applications of soot and potash from the ashes of his bonfire and using organic pyrethrums as an insect repellent made from effusions of plants, or the use of their nitrate fixing properties and the many other Victorian remedies he had learnt as a boy in rural Devon. The abundance of garden produce and fruit saw their way onto our table and we ate well, supplementing the scarce rationing of the day. He inherited from his predecessor a fig tree planted against the south facing wall of the garden which he expertly pruned and which produced large, very desirable, purple figs of an incredibly sweet and sticky nature which attracted all the wasps of the neighbourhood. The vine in the conservatory also benefited from his attentions and produced prolific bunches of purple grapes which were mostly used for dessert; but a few went into his supply of home made wine.

Cooking was another of his hobbies and curries were his speciality which he had learnt to make when in India. He had acquired the ingredients in 1946, when he had gone out to fetch my blind grandmother back from India after her husband had died there. He had brought back supplies of tamarind, turmeric and many other spices that were simply not obtainable in England then. He would seem to throw the ingredients into the pan with abandon and without recourse to a recipe book, and this applied to whatever else he was cooking, but despite this apparent casualness, his meals always turned out well and were very tasty. His cooking interests were in savouries and what might be described as real puddings, those which had some body to them, suet based or otherwise solid, and he was not interested in cake making which remained Auntie's speciality.

Both Uncle and Auntie loved pets and, as a useful handyman with hammer and nails, he built two large aviaries for his singing canaries and the budgerigars which he bred. He would never have made a joiner, being far too quick in his execution of projects for finesse. The other pets of the household were a tortoise and the huge, short-coated, tabby tom-cat called Winkie, who took pride of place on the best of the household armchairs and could only be dislodged if you allowed him to sit on your lap.

Winkie was a top cat and courted all the local females with considerable noise, but he had a rival, an equally large black Persian whose long coat made him appear even larger. These two were well matched and their fights over lady friends or territory were frightening to watch and were often only stopped when they were caught in a position where a bucket of water could be thrown over them. If anyone thought cats were not formidable, these battles would have soon disillusioned them and woe betide any mere human who got entangled in their disputes. Because they were so well matched, neither one of them ever achieved final dominance and over the years their ears got more and more ragged and their faces became progressively more scarred. Winkie would often come in with open wounds seeping blood which needed immediate disinfection and attention and sometimes stitches. It is no joke to see the end result of a serious fight between two large tom cats; and why people in those days did not have them neutered is a mystery.

When we had exhausted all the possibilities of exploration, we engaged on a project to build a go-cart. Ours consisted of a wooden fruit box, big enough to sit in with knees drawn up to the chin, with a main longitudinal plank which formed the chassis, onto one end of which the box seat was secured and which, at the other end, had a short plank fixed across it at right angles, pivoted at the centre to act as a steering arm. Beneath the steering arm and the box seat was a set of wheels and axles, which we had dismantled from a discarded pram found on a dump. The steering arm had cord fixed to its ends so that pulling on either string would turn the cart one way or the other. The whole thing was put together with nails and one bolt for the steering arm pivot. One of us would sit in while the other pushed down the gentle slope of the road leading to the creek, and when sufficient momentum had been reached, the pusher would jump with both feet onto the back axle. It worked well but relied on shoe leather for brakes and so was not very popular with the adults. The prototype did not last very long, with the contraption breaking its back, as the nails pulled out when the pusher jumped on for one last turn. Later we persuaded Uncle to let us have some screws, which made a more lasting job after the essential repairs.

Our ventures continued with a home-made yacht whose hull we constructed from layers of wooden date box bottoms nailed together. We adopted this method because we could cut the outlines with the fretsaw Harvey had been given the previous Christmas, where we would have had more difficulty with carving from the solid wood. The sails were very crude hand-sewn off-cuts from old pillow cases. All this had been inspired by watching the old sea-dogs sailing their one metre yachts, but I am afraid ours was unseaworthy and the real pleasure lay in the making. We did have a much more satisfactory outcome with the very cheap, tinplate, put-put, steam motor boat we had acquired, which had a boiler pan from which two copper pipes ran to discharge out of the stern of the boat. When a candle was lit under the primed boiler, steam bubbles would emerge in quick succession from the one pipe making a rapid put-put noise, hence the name, while presumably a much slower entry of replacement water took place in the other pipe. The explosive exit of the steam would drive the boat forward in a slow circular path.

Not all our time was spent in fun and games. Apart from chores such as washing up, we had the duty of reading back the letters that blind Grannie had so laboriously typed. We would hear her touch typing with a very regular slow rhythm, worthy of a metronome, as she tried to make certain that no errors crept into her work. On one occasion she presented me with a full page, which had taken her a considerable time to type, and all that I could see was utter gibberish, as she had misplaced her fingering from the very start. She had a huge circulation of friends with whom she corresponded and this filled the void in her life that her blindness had brought about. We were fascinated by her various routines to help her cope and watched as she lined up papers and carbons, and carefully felt for the correct position to place them into the typewriter rollers, and then felt the edge of the paper to set the margins.

She had a large number of Braille books from the lending library of the RNIB, and a set of the Gospels which were her own, and we would be called on to help her locate the one she next wanted to read. She was extremely methodical and it was not often that she got them muddled, and she would tell us on which shelf, and how many books along, was the one she needed. We had also to be very circumspect, as she had enhanced hearing and would hear us even when we crept to some spot in the room where we might be interested in something that had caught our attention. She would immediately want to know what we were doing. We were often called upon to count the stitches on her knitting needles, or to read to her newspapers and stories which were not obtainable in her Braille library. Her taste in books was not ours and we would do our best to pass the buck to the other brother, or find some excuse to avoid the chore, but she was part of our limited family with Mother and Father away and we were fond of her and would not have deliberately denied her demands.

Sunday was not an easy day for the two of us as we were expected to attend the morning service at Middlecroft Gospel Hall, return for lunch and then walk back for Sunday School, return for tea and finally go back for the evening Gospel Service. The morning service was a devotional service of hymns, prayers and Bible readings followed by the breaking of bread, more familiarly known as the communion by other denominations. Participation in the communion part of the service was only for those who had experienced baptism by full immersion in water. The Gospel Service was a lively affair with rousing hymns and would be taken by a preacher whose message would always proclaim the way of salvation. In addition to this there was one midweek evening meeting for Bible Study that we had to attend. It was while waiting at the bus stop for the bus to take us to this service, that we were picked on by a couple of boys of our own age, and it ended by an exchange of one punch each by me and the older boy, before both parties decided to walk away in opposite directions and we did not attend the Bible Class that night. I am not sure what I said to Uncle to explain our non attendance but he wisely did not insist that we went back that evening. I think he guessed that we had had a severe fright.

The holiday was split up into chunks so that we were not too much of a burden to Uncle and Auntie and so we were sent next to Uncle Fred and Auntie Olive, living in Edgeware in the London suburbs, and then on to Auntie Mary. Uncle Fred was Father's third brother and Auntie Mary was the youngest of the family who lived in Newcastle-on-Tyne. She was married to Uncle David, a surgeon who had been parachuted behind the lines into German occupied Yugoslavia during the war, in order to work with the partisans. Much later he was to become Professor of Surgery at Durban's King Edward VIII Hospital in South Africa where, in his spare time, he made himself an expert in snake venom and became an international authority on this subject. He would be called on to lecture at conferences all over the world. His adventurous lifestyle and his Ronald Coleman good looks made him a very fine catch for Auntie Mary and complemented her own red-haired beauty and warm nature and social skills. Invitations to their home in Durban were much sought after. When we visited them in Newcastle they were very young and not very well off and had just started a family with their nine month old daughter Christine. Auntie Mary was very kind to us and they both took a great deal of trouble to assimilate us in all their outdoor activities, which included rambles on the moors and picnics. When they later had a Morris Minor, Uncle tuned the engine and suspension and started rallying. We would accompany him in this mildly souped-up car, but the numerous hill climbs he entered often saw his clutch burnt out.

The journey up to Newcastle had its hazards with the inevitable change of trains from the Waterloo terminus of the Southern Railway to that at Kings Cross for the LNER east coast expresses to the north. I was only eleven and, unaccompanied, had no idea that the invitingly empty coach on the Newcastle express that we had got into, had been labelled Grimsby. The train gathered speed through the tunnels and canyons of the backs of the tall city terraces and factories and by the time we were passing through the outer suburbs we were going at a cracking speed, with the thunderous noise of a heavily loaded Gresley locomotive and its four cylinder beat, as it pulled up the inclines near Potters Bar.

The country began to open up and we soon realised that the east coast expresses went far faster than the GWR train we took to Birmingham, with telegraph poles going by in a blur and the hypnotic rhythm slowly nodding us to sleep. When I woke up, I had no knowledge that the train had stopped at some intermediate station in Yorkshire and our two coaches had been uncoupled and reconnected to a local train now heading east. We sat on in ignorance until we arrived at a station with the name board Grimsby and wondered why the train seemed to remain there for longer than usual. Finally a guard wandered up the train, slamming doors and came upon us. He told us that we had reached our destination and should get off as the train went no further. When he saw that our tickets were for Newcastle, he told us that we should not have been on these coaches, which had been left behind by the mainline express, and that we would have to catch the next train to York in an hour's time and change there for Newcastle. He shepherded us into the waiting room and later found two ladies who were going to York and asked them to see that we got there safely. These two ladies saw a pair of very tired and frightened boys and they mothered us. They bought us buns and a mug of tea from the station buffet, and when we were finally on the train, we found ourselves nodding off to sleep, with an arm around us and our heads leaning against a comforting shoulder. The guard had telephoned ahead to let Auntie know what had happened and someone at York ensured that we got on the right train for Newcastle. We were collected at the station and taken home to a very late tea and an early bed.

The holidays ended with us returning to Gosport just before the start of term and with our being kitted out with the usual equipment that needed replacement, or which we had grown out of. We were sent back to school, as always, with a large tin containing Auntie's boiled fruit cake.

21. Seasoned Schoolboy

All the talk that autumn of 1947 was of the forthcoming Royal Wedding. Princess Elizabeth was going to marry her sweetheart Philip Mountbatten. He had been a Lieutenant in the Royal Navy when, as a young teenager, she fell head over heels in love with him. But why had the Royal family picked the dark and dreary month of November? Maybe they thought that it would cheer us up during that period when the nation was at its lowest ebb, with few if any consumer goods in the shops and with a massive war debt hanging over it. The excitement among the staff was much more palpable than amongst the boys, who would only have been able to appreciate the significance of the event at the time it took place. The senior staff had arranged weeks before to rent a large-screen television for the occasion and this would be placed in the staffroom. Celebration fireworks were purchased and a special menu prepared for the staff and those boarders who would be remaining at school. An official holiday had been declared and the dayboys would all be at home for the great day, but they and their parents were invited to return to the school for the fireworks display. There would of course have been the alternative of municipal fireworks displays being shown in all the parks throughout the land and many would prefer to attend these with their much grander shows.

When it arrived, it was a day of great joy and friendship, with strangers greeting each other as pals. Furniture had been pushed to one side and all the boys who had not gone home were packed into the staffroom to sit on the floor in front of the hired television screen. The staff sat on chairs behind. The set was switched on and it seemed an age before the picture very slowly emerged from the background, as the large thermionic valves warmed up, and the coarse lines of an early 405 line set gradually expanded from a miniature black and white picture to fill the whole of the screen. The set itself had an enormous mahogany cabinet and the whole thing gave out a background hum that is not apparent in modern TVs. It was the first time I had ever seen television and I was not to experience it again until 1966 when, married with a young family, we bought one of those appallingly unreliable, dual-standard black and white sets for the World Cup. Their unreliability stemmed from the huge bussbar, which clunked across with a great thump, as it changed the multitude of contacts to enable either the outgoing 405 line or the new 625 line standard picture to be shown. Not only were contacts formed like this poor, but a regular succession of bangs were never going to be appreciated by the fragile valves.

The wedding itself seemed to have an emotional impact on the lady members of the staff and even to us boys, the pomp, solemnity and brilliance of the well rehearsed ceremony made a deep impression. Princess Elizabeth was very much loved by everyone and it seemed as if we were taking part in the wedding of a family that was well known to us. Cameos remain of King George VI leaving the Royal Coach with his very young and beautiful daughter on his arm and later of this same young Princess being helped into the same coach with a young and extremely handsome Naval Officer as her new husband, to be proudly shown to the whole world as they drove from the Abbey to the Mall. Then there was the pageantry of the parade, with the immaculate Guards on horseback in their brilliant uniforms, sparkling after the drab khaki of the wartime troops, and the Guards were followed by the contrasting dark uniforms of the naval bluejackets and their white blancoed webbing. Familiar pictures of the Royal Family waving from the Palace balcony to the densely packed crowds in the Mall come to mind. It all seemed to go on for a very long time and at the end of the day, in the dark of the early November evening, there were the fireworks to watch, and not only one's own, but those of the neighbours whose rockets rose high into the night sky.

At some stage during the following summer the restrictions on the use of electricity were removed and the whole of England went out to view the towns and villages as they were lit up. It was so unusual an event that Mr Peacock made a special dispensation so that all the boys could be marched into Solihull High Street to see the lights come on: no prep for any of us that night. This was perhaps the first real indication that Britain had at last emerged from the war, though rationing of food and clothes would go on for some time and only in 1952, four years later and long after Germany had removed her own restrictions, would we see the last of this rationing. It must be difficult for people now to imagine what it was like to have everywhere dark as soon as the sun went down and to have all the shop windows black. And another touch to signal the end of the gloom under which we had lived for so long, was the birth of His Royal Highness Prince Charles to Princess Elizabeth and Prince Philip in November 1948.

Late in the summer of 1948, the school Cub Pack went camping on a farm at Kings Norton, where there was a substantial stream running through the field in which the tents were set. Kings Norton nowadays is completely built up and I have no idea where this could have been. It is just possible that the area shown on the present maps as Staplehall Farm Recreation Ground, with the river Rea running through, was the site. All I know was that it was a working farm, and that we collected milk and eggs for the troop from it. Alongside the camping field was a wood also straddling the river.

We slept in groups of about six boys each, in substantial

canvas ridge tents, and were woken early in the morning for our ablutions in bowls of water taken directly from the river. Breakfast followed, with porridge distributed from large metal pans hung over an open wood fire on tripods made from branches. It had been cooked by us under supervision and we made good use of the demonstrations on lashings that we had been given earlier in the year, in the Cub Pack, to make these tripods. Mr Elliot demonstrated how to cook scrambled eggs, which he made for himself and Miss Glazebrook in a large frying pan over the fire, and he then left us to get on with our own. Toast and tea followed, with the toast being made by skewering bread on a sharpened stick and offering it up to the fire. Many a slice dropped into the embers and came out as a charred offering, which had to be scraped and eaten, as Mr Elliot was not going to issue a new slice to compensate for incompetence. Even burnt toast tasted wonderful when cooked in the open and, no doubt, the fresh air and constant outdoor activity sharpened our appetites.

At the end of the first day we had a camp song. Gathered round the campfire, there were many verses that began with the opening line, 'Kings Norton in the mud...', all sung to a well known rugby tune. That first full day was hot and, for decency, we were sent into the wood to change into our swimming trunks away from the eyes of Miss Glazebrook. The tents were too small and low for us to change in easily. We then entered into a free for all, paddling and splashing and throwing mud but finally we emerged clean from the water and dried out in the sun. It was when we were changing that I noticed for the first time that some of the boys were showing the early signs of puberty and when I looked down at myself, I saw also the first indications of developing body hair. I had been completely unaware of sex up to that point and we were not given any instruction in the subject. Now we began to talk about it but we were totally uninformed and could only make guesses as to what was happening.

Seasoned Schoolboy

Not long after this we became much more aware of these changes. It was normal practice to have allocated bath nights at school, where a batch of us would go through the three or so baths we had and would then dry and get into our pyjamas ready for bed. This activity would be supervised by Matron or one of her assistants, most of whom were older ladies and had seen it all before and were totally indifferent. But about this time, Matron had acquired a new assistant straight from school, Miss Murdoch*, a very young Scots girl probably no more than sixteen or seventeen years old, with apple cheeks on a white face and that luxuriant dark brown hair that a lot of Scots lassies have. She could be made to blush on the slightest pretext and I believe she was very naive and innocent. She was usually accompanied by Matron when it was her turn to supervise our bath nights, but on this one occasion, Matron was delayed and Miss Murdoch had been left on her own. Most of us, even though showing the first indications of puberty, were not in any way sexually developed but this was not so for Littlemore*, who must have been at least eighteen months ahead of us in his development. He was endowed with a full adult complement of male parts and these were of generous proportions. Miss Murdoch must have been fascinated by what was inadvertently on display and when he came for the towel on the towel rail by her, she could not suppress her extreme curiosity. She reached down to his genitals and ever so gently cupped his testicles in her hand and felt their weight. The next moment she was running out of the bathroom, slowly suffusing with a deepening scarlet as she went, until her face, her arms, her legs and every uncovered part of her was now this startling hue. We were so astonished by the suddenness of what we had witnessed that we had no time to react to this astounding sexual stimulus or even to consider what the impact would have been on poor Littlemore. Though nobody reported

---

*Murdoch and Littlemore are substitute names.

the incident, she must have felt that she would need to change her job and she left shortly after.

Once again fate determined that I should not see the end of this Cub Camp. My tonsils had become infected numerous times since coming to England and, with the introduction of Bevin's new National Health Service, I now qualified for a free operation for their removal. A bed had become available while I was at camp and I had to leave immediately for the hospital. I do not remember much about it, except for my convalescence in the school sick bay, where I was fed on a diet largely consisting of jelly and ice cream. I had no complaints! My idle hours were spent making beautifully detailed, miniature, cut-out cardboard, model aeroplanes carefully folded and glued along the seams with balsa wood cement. The models we made were of the latest British and American jets, Meteors, Vampires and Sabre Jets and their rival Russian MIGs. My fellow convalescents and I would sneak over to each other's beds when Matron had left, in order to conduct mock aerial battles with our assorted planes.

Half term was a problem, with us having to stay at school when everyone else was home for the long weekend, and it meant that a member of staff would have to look after us. Often this would be Mr Coleman, the master who took us to the Plymouth Brethren meeting. It was not long before Lloyd, a boy whose father was vicar of St Thomas' church in Stourbridge, had told his parents of our situation and we were invited to spend the break at the vicarage. I remember more about the train journey across the heart of the West Midlands conurbation than the stay, but I do remember a walk to the Hagley Monument. It was one of those Victorian follies that abound and in this case it bore a resemblance to Cleopatra's Needle. The whole thing was in a state of great decay and was quite unsafe to go near. We circumnavigated it at a distance and with considerable care.

For subsequent half terms, Dad had used his network of Plymouth Brethren contacts to arrange for us to spend these breaks with Mr and Mrs White at Stafford. Mr White was an Income Tax Inspector nearing his retirement and was the epitomy of integrity. His wife was a very fine cook and they always followed tradition by having a roast beef and Yorkshire pudding lunch on Sunday, with roast potatoes and quantities of very rich stock gravy made from the drippings of the thickly fat encrusted joint. I ate this roast with relish but always ended up with a bilious attack and a terrible headache. With hindsight I am sure this was a migraine brought on by an upset tummy so unused to such a rich diet.

Our favourite activity from their home was to walk down to the railway tracks at Stafford junction. This was one of the major junctions of the Midlands where the Euston west coast line met up with the lines from the south passing through Birmingham and Wolverhampton. The engines were in the maroon colours of the LMS, as opposed to the green GWR locos which we normally saw. There was always plenty of activity to watch and it kept us from being under the feet of Mr and Mrs White for long periods of time.

We would often walk into Stafford town centre and make a beeline for Woolworths. It was here that I committed my second major sin. We always needed sandpaper and Woolworths sold it for a penny halfpenny a sheet. Unfortunately I had spent all my pocket money and so I just took the sandpaper and walked out of the shop. I had not walked more than ten paces when I was stopped by a shop assistant and asked to come back in to see the Manager. I was asked why I had not paid for it and when I said that I had no money, the Manager wanted to phone my Father, but he soon learnt my position and sent me back, saying that he would contact Mr White. I felt so ashamed that, despite my very strict upbringing, I had stolen something and would bring disgrace on my family and particularly my Mother. I crept back with dragging footsteps to the house to face the music and I was particularly scared of Mr White and his probity. He must have guessed how I was feeling because, though very stern, he did not moralise but made it quite clear that we were all entitled to one chance to redeem ourselves and that there would not be a second one. The Manager had said to him that as this was my first offence, he was not going to take any further action. It took many years for me to live with this disgrace and overcome the recurring nightmares.

My little band of friends were now in the last year at Eversfield and had reached the age of twelve where we were the most senior boys in the school. This was the age when we first became aware of girls, those strange creatures that we only saw at a distance when we were taken into town. Some boys had sisters at home and to them girls were no mystery, but for the rest of us they were a different species whose interests and behaviour were quite unlike ours. Perhaps it was this enigma that aroused our curiosity and the fact that, on those rare occasions when our paths crossed, they whispered amongst themselves while looking at us and breaking into giggles. They seemed to have a vivaciousness that required no purpose, which was in contrast to our much more serious and intently focused outpourings of energy in the pursuit of a task. And, not least of all, many of them were quite pretty.

One of these rare occasions when we would come across them was at the combined Crusader meeting held each school term in central Birmingham at the Friends Meeting House, rented for the purpose. Crusaders was an interdenominational movement aimed at promoting Christianity to the school-age young people of this country in a fun way, which included summer camps. Many schools had Crusader Classes and, at that time, these were separate for boys and girls. It was only at the Friends Meeting House that they came together. This building was the headquarters of the Quaker movement in the West Midlands and we met in the large hall which had a gallery round three sides. Because there were far more boys than girls, the floor of the hall was filled with boys. All the girls sat together in one of the side arms of the gallery and we happened to be sitting in the opposite arm. I had a girlfriend called Helen Richards and we made eyes at each other across the gallery, before shyness would make us look away and then, when we had regained our composure, we would have another surreptitious exchange of glances.

Helen was the sister of one of the younger boys. She was a dark eyed girl who resembled illustrations of Shakespeare's Ann Hathaway. My group decided that she should be allocated to me after much discussion amongst ourselves, as had other sisters to the rest of the group. I had never met Helen, but she had been told of this arrangement by her brother and I had been described to her; and a certain amount of pointing at the Crusader meeting had confirmed identities. Following this first contact, young Richards, who was not averse to the conspiracy, was asked by the group to arrange for his parents to invite me to lunch one Sunday. After the Sunday service his father arrived in a black Austin Sheerline car and drove us both to the family home in the neighbouring village of Dorridge, where I was introduced to Helen as though neither of us had any previous knowledge of each other. The meal proved to be a success and of course there were the usual shy glances across the table but our relationship developed no further. I had no idea what to say to girls and the whole affair had been arranged and was not the natural outcome of a mutual attraction. In fact my main memory of the occasion was the impression created by the brand new Austin Sheerline which, with the Austin Princess, were the flagship motors of the Longbridge car factory. They both shared the same very large body with enormous headlights more akin to searchlights, but I believe the Princess had a slightly higher specification. For several years afterwards one would see these two models used as wedding cars or converted as hearses for use in funeral processions. My experiment with the fair sex was over and I had to wait a few more years before it was renewed.

22. Family Holiday

My time at Eversfield was over. Mother and Father had returned to England on furlough after their three year stint in Malaya and we could look forward to a glorious six months together as a family. This family now included our sister Else, who had been born the previous year and was now nearly a year and a half old.

Father arrived at the end of the summer term in a brand new black Hillman Minx of ultra modern design. Gone were the chassis and separate wings of pre-war cars: this was monocoque design. Laimbeer's father arrived in a black Packard. Both cars caused a sensation; one because it was enormous and American; the other because it was streamlined and because English people could not get new cars. Every car made here was sent for export to earn those foreign currencies that Britain so badly needed after being bankrupted during the war. Father qualified for one because he was a colonial civil servant who would be taking his car abroad with him, when shortly he returned to Malaya. All the cars of that era were black and ours was no exception.

We were going to travel to the Trossachs in Scotland, to Callander where Chrissie McIntyre's aunt lived with her elderly husband, Mr McArthur. Chrissie McIntyre was an Australian nurse who during the war had served in India, staying at the Coonoor YWCA, where she became Mother's closest friend. She had told Mother that we must visit her uncle and aunt when we returned to England, hence this visit. Three years earlier we had

had to travel everywhere on public transport and it was not practical, at that time, to get to Callander so far north and with such a crowded schedule.

There were no motorways in those days and Father was going to do the near four hundred mile journey in one day. What he had not anticipated was that there might be problems with a brand new car which had only just been run in. We set off from the Midlands in grand style and it was not long before we were hurtling along at sixty miles an hour on the open roads, a speed that I had never experienced before and which seemed like flying. Even new cars, then, had inadequate drum brakes and thin cross-ply tyres that made steering and road holding difficult, and progress at these speeds meant a continual series of small steering corrections which had the car wandering either side of the desired line. After a couple of hours, Father found that each time he wanted power on a hill or he wanted to accelerate and stepped hard on the accelerator, nothing happened. If however he built up his speed gradually, the car would behave impeccably. This was fine until he came to the next hill when he would have to go down to the lowest gears and proceed up it at a crawl. The two garages he called at both diagnosed dirty fuel and cleaned out the carburettor but to no effect. The result of all this was that we were getting later and later and would have to complete a considerable part of the journey after dark, despite it being the height of summer. Then to add to his troubles, when he switched on the lights, he found that the battery was not being charged and the lights gradually got dimmer and dimmer. He dared not stop as the battery would not have enough charge left to re-start the engine. We eventually got in at around midnight to the dismay of our elderly hosts, who were in their seventies and who normally went to bed on the dot of ten.

The garage in Callander had the car in for a whole day and found that the dynamo belt was slipping and so not charging the battery; and that the carburettor main jet had a flap of swarf from the machining that was sucked into the jet on high fuel demand, thus blocking it. When the fuel demand lessened, it sprang back and unblocked the jet allowing the car to run normally. It was soon put right.

The old man, Mr McArthur, was as tough a Highlander as you could wish to see, lean and sinewy, and proposed that he would lead us all on a walk up Ben Leddi, a mountain of over three thousand feet behind the town. Sadly, I had developed a very severe migraine with all the stress of the previous day's journey and had also suffered from car sickness, to which I was prone when a boy, so that for me, the climb was out of the question, despite my love of walking on the mountains. I was very envious of Harvey who never suffered from travel sickness and who went on to complete the climb.

From this three day visit we went on to Belfast, once more to stay with Uncle Albin and Auntie Grace. We settled in happily, as Uncle was another of that generation who were mad on trains, and not only had he many framed pen and ink drawings of them on his walls, which he had drawn, some in colour, but he had a comprehensive '00'-gauge railway layout in the loft, which we were allowed to use under supervision. He was skilled at this pen and ink drawing and had first met Auntie at Art Class. She was recognised as a talented amateur artist and from this the romance had developed.

Uncle also possessed the highest level kit of Meccano that the factory made. With this we made a working pantograph which produced various geometric designs on a circular sheet of paper. This was achieved by a pencil fixed to an arm of variable radius, which moved relative to the rotating sheet of paper on the turntable. The interaction of these two separate motions made for a seemingly infinite variety of patterns. We also made a giant model of a dockside crane, the only snag being that, when we asked for help because of the extreme complexity of the design details, Uncle would get very enthusiastic and take over from us.

By now their eldest daughter Hazel-Mary was of school age and had to be escorted there by Auntie. We were press-ganged into taking over this duty, which entailed walking the mile to the school with Hazel-Mary sitting on the saddle of Auntie's bicycle, which we pushed. We did not mind pushing the bike but we slunk along hoping that no other boys of our age group would see us with a young girl on the bike. We would have been taunted all the way there and back.

Mother had done some very interesting shopping in Belfast and she was very mysterious about it. We guessed that it concerned us and when she was out of the room, we raided her handbag and found two very smart, new, black fountain pens in presentation cases which were obviously for us. We removed them and examined them in great detail, pulling out the refill lever and unscrewing the tops and the barrels. When we were satisfied with our examination, we replaced everything as before. We did this on a couple of occasions and then, perhaps because we had not replaced everything in exactly the right place, Mother became suspicious and they disappeared from her handbag. We were eventually to get them at the beginning of the next school term.

We must have explored most of Belfast by bus and with the loan of bikes and had made friends with some of the neighbours' children. Joy of joys, one of the boys in the same road had an air gun which neither of us had ever used. He was very generous, giving us a handful of pellets, and we spent a happy half hour shooting at various targets in his garden with limited success. Other activities, of the ten days or so we spent in Belfast, included a memorable visit to the Belfast Air Show. We saw at close quarters some of Britain's experimental aircraft, including the prototype of the Fleet Air Arm's latest contra-prop plane, the Fairey Gannet. Deep bellied, with its twin engines within the body, it was squat and powerful looking, with a double gull wing fold to its wings. We also saw many of the famous wartime bombers and fighters, but perhaps the most interesting of these was the Sunderland Flying Boat, which was open for a detailed inspection. We were allowed to sit in the pilot's seat and try out the controls and we could move into the double deck working area, galley and crew's quarters and try out their bunks. Moored near the airstrip was an old aircraft carrier, converted from a large merchant ship, which the public were allowed to clamber all over and this provided further interest.

Both families now moved down to the farm near Annsboro where we had stayed three years previously. From here we visited and climbed Sleive Donnard and Sleive Binion in the mountains of Mourne and looked down the Silent Valley onto the huge reservoirs that supplied Belfast with water. We explored the coast and took a trip over the border to Dundalk and worked our way up through Newcastle and on to Strangford Lough, as on the previous holiday three years earlier.

We had arrived at the time of harvest and Harvey and I joined in the work of collecting the tied sheaves of corn and placing them in four sheaf conical stooks with the ears of corn at the top, so that the wind could blow through and dry them. The cutting machine, known as a binder, was towed behind a small Ferguson tractor and had a rotating windmill flail that dropped the cut stalks onto a wide canvas belt, where they were then taken up to rotating metal arms which gathered them into bundles. These were then tied with binder twine and more arms threw these bundles over the side for us to collect. The binder twine was made from coarse vegetable fibre and was the farmer's complete do-it-yourself kit: it was used for everything. Flax was another prolific product of the farms of Northern Ireland and this was cut and set to soak in watery ditches where it gave off the most noxious of smells as we drove past. The long fibres remaining after the decomposition of the softer vegetable

Family Holiday

Blake, Harvey, Else and the horse from which Harvey fell and broke his wrist.

matter would be woven into the linen for which Ireland was famous.

In addition to his Ferguson tractor, the farmer still used a giant carthorse for some tasks and this animal was kept in the field at the end of the farm drive, when he was not required for duty. The field had a high bank adjacent to the gate and Harvey had worked out a way of mounting the horse. He persuaded it to come to him with some juicy handfuls of grass and when it was close enough, he jumped off the bank on to its back and with his rapport with animals, was able to get it to walk around the field. I followed suit, but it would only stand still for me. Perhaps it was because I was a lot bigger and a lot plumper than Harvey and the horse did not like the extra weight. This became a daily routine until one day Harvey, who could not easily straddle such a wide back, slipped off in mid-field and landed heavily on his wrist. The wrist was broken and it had to be put in plaster.

Dad must have thought that we needed to learn what it was like to carry out a task that required self discipline to see it through. He had acquired an old pushchair for Else and had decided that it would look a lot better for a coat of paint. All his family were perfectionists and, for him, this meant that the pushchair would have to be sanded down to gleaming bare metal before restoration. There were no chemical paint strippers then, and the only way to do this was by the application of elbow grease and emery cloth. In front of the farmhouse was a south facing lawn where we were sat in the sunshine on an old sheet, surrounded by bits of pram stripped down as far as it would go. We rubbed and rubbed until the emery cloth got less and less efficient as it clogged up with old paint, and the mounting pile of completed parts was finally ready to be inspected by Dad. We hated the job, especially when we came to clean the coil springs which provided the pram's suspension. You could only do these by threading a thin strip of emery cloth round the spring and see-sawing the two ends of cloth back and forth. The job went on in half hour stints for two or three days until Harvey's fortuitous broken wrist brought it to an end. Either Dad had given up on us ever completing the job, or he must have felt that it was not fair that I should be the sole worker. At least that was the end of the affair and I believe the pram was painted gloss black by Dad without any further stripping. It was a case of 'Do as I say but not as I do'.

As to our sister, an eighteen month old baby did not impact much on the busy lives of two boys of twelve and eleven and apart from the pram incident, which drew our attention to her existence, she seemed almost an irrelevance. I hasten to add that later in our lives she became very much more appreciated.

So the holidays came to an end and I was to start at a new school. I had ceased to be the young English boy from abroad, observing England through foreign eyes. I no longer grieved over my lost past in India, and its freedoms, and I had become fully integrated into English ways and attitudes. From this point on I spent the next five years as a very ordinary schoolboy, at a school near Bath, with a story that many English people would easily recognise.

Postscript

In 1954 I began my two years National Service in the Royal Navy as an Ordinary Seaman and then later was made up to an Able Seaman. I was one of the very lucky ones who was sent out first to Gibraltar and Malta, then briefly touched on Greece, as we delivered relief supplies to the victims of the Argostoli earthquake, and later we passed on through the Suez Canal via Aden to Singapore. My next eighteen months were spent in the Far East Fleet on the Admiral's flagship, HMS *Newfoundland*, a cruiser armed with three turrets of nine six-inch guns and many four-inch and smaller calibre guns. We called at every destination from Korea and Japan to Australia including the Philippines, Hong Kong, Bangkok, Malaya, Singapore, Borneo and Fremantle and finally flew home to be demobbed just before the Suez crisis. I had somehow also just missed the Korean war, though we were closed up at action stations all the time we were off the Korean coast, and the only action I saw was when we were cruising off the western Malayan coast lobbing six-inch shells on the Chinese communist guerrilla camps in the jungle. We were firing at random intervals so that they would not detect a pattern and would be suitably demoralised. When a ship fires large calibre shells the whole of the hull jumps. We had just sat down to our lunch when this happened and the light bulb over the mess table shattered into tiny shards of glass which floated down into our food. I am not sure who was the most demoralised, us or the communists.

I spent three years at university studying engineering, married a girl I had met there while a student, started a family and from then on lived in a most conventional way. I worked in water engineering, engaged on schemes from the Reservoir to the Sewage Purification Works, the refining processes of which might well be an allegory of my life from the cradle to retirement. It has been a good life!